REDCAPS

POLICING THE ARMY

REDCAPS

POLICING THE ARMY

ROGER MILLS AND KEVIN MANN

In association with Mann Made Films
based on the BBC TV programme

BⓉXTREE

First published in Great Britain in 1995 by Boxtree Limited
by arrangement with BBC Worldwide Limited

Text © Roger Mills and Kevin Mann 1995
Photographs © Kevin Mann 1995 (with the exception of pages 8, 13, 14, 15, 124, 125 courtesy of BBC
Worldwide Limited; 21, 37, 38, 39, 55 top and bottom, 101, 102, 104, 106, 108 top and bottom, 111
courtesy of the Royal Military Police)

10 9 8 7 6 5 4 3 2 1

Designed by Design 23
Printed and bound in Great Britain by Bath Press Colour Books, Glasgow, for

Boxtree Limited
Broadwall House
21 Broadwall
London   SE1 9PL

A CIP catalogue entry for this book is available from the British Library.

ISBN 1 85283 909 0

Front cover photograph courtesy of BBC Worldwide Limited
Back cover photograph courtesy of the Royal Military Police

CONTENTS

'When you put the red cap on, you become part of something that represents the highest of standards. You must remain beyond reproach at all times and follow our motto, Exemplo Ducemus – "By example shall we lead".
– Training Instructor

ACKNOWLEDGMENTS

Books on the military tend to be written by servicemen. It is not often that the layman has sufficient access to write anything worthwhile. As television producers, we have been in the unusual position of being allowed behind all sorts of closed doors in the interests of researching our series. This book is drawn from that material.

We are extremely grateful to the RMP personnel who opened those doors for us, without their leap of faith we would not have made the series. We are also particularly indebted to Col. T.G. Scriven who endorsed our original approach and stuck with us through thick and thin. We are unstintingly grateful to Maj. Bill Trundley, the man in the middle, who deflected the Green Machine's flak, and who guided our stumbling footsteps through the military minefield. Also to Maj. Frank Lindop, Capt. John Wooldridge, Sgt Sean O'Brien and all the incredibly hard-working corporals of the Royal Military Police who were prepared to allow us into their world.

The Redcaps mean different things to different people. The convoy that got through will bless them. The squaddies, picked up as they painted the town red, will curse them. We describe the Redcaps as we saw and heard them. The errors in this book are all ours.

SMOKESCREENS

This was the television series the Army did not want. It was approved at the highest level, by the Minister of Defence no less, and there was even a signed piece of paper to prove it. But between approval and access, cracks appeared, followed by a chasm.

The Green Machine, those middle and senior officers who stoically implement the decisions of the civil servants and the politicians, had not been consulted. It was as if the Army's political masters had gone day-dreaming into a contract, the implications of which had not been thought through.

As C-Day approached, when the cameras would start to roll, those implications began to sink in. The awful truth was that while the Royal Military Police, also known as the RMP or Redcaps, might benefit from exposure in a six-part series for the BBC, there was 'nothing in it for the Army'. In fact, quite the reverse. By dwelling exclusively on the work of the RMP, the Army would be represented only by its miscreants, its drunkards, its fraudsters and its criminals.

The Army reflects the society from which it is drawn. The fact that it is predominantly male and in the eighteen to thirty age group has a bearing on its overall behaviour. It is probably no more lawless than a similar group of people in civilian life, but by concentrating on the RMP, an outfit that spends one hundred per cent of its time policing the least attractive ten per cent of the Army, the image that would emerge week after week could only be highly detrimental, or so it was argued.

The British Army has a unique structure. It is composed of little mafias called regiments, and presiding over each regiment is a benign despot called a Commanding Officer, or CO, of lieutenant-colonel rank. Like all such groups a regiment is tight-knit, and it does not like its dirty linen washed in public. The code of *omerta* prevails.

For many officers becoming colonel of his regiment is the fulfilment of a lifetime's ambition. The officer holds the position for only two years, but he has had to excel in the Army's complicated command structure. When he achieves the long-coveted goal – particularly if the regiment is a famous one with a long pedigree – it is almost a sacred trust.

These are highly motivated and intelligent men. As a new CO dines in the mess with his brother officers, the long table brilliant with regimental silver, the walls flickering in the candlelight that picks out oil paintings of dashing cavalry charges still green in the regimental memory, he feels an almost mystic sense of his place in the continuum of things. He also feels the weight of contemporary pressures, and is aware of former COs still living who are monitoring his performance, and who will censure him for anything that tarnishes the regiment's reputation during his tenure.

Opposite: The proud, public face of the Army at a Second World War remembrance parade in York.

It was the trust and cooperation of men such as these that the makers of the series would have to gain, if the venture was to succeed. But what possible argument could any outsider advance to a man who had clawed his way up the Army triangle of promotion, who for two years holds the baton of command with almost superstitious awe, and whose prospects for promotion to brigadier depend so critically on his conduct over those two years?

There were two further obstacles. The RMP have never been liked; accepted as a regrettable necessity perhaps, but loved, no. They are the Army's policemen. When they arrive, it means trouble. When they arrive trailed by a BBC film crew, it means double trouble. The crime the RMP is investigating cannot be contained – it will be on display to a wider audience, to the great British viewing public.

The second obstacle was the Army's own attitude to the media. At best it is prepared to give them the benefit of the doubt until its worst suspicions are confirmed. At worst it is hostile and mistrustful, if always polite. Asked the reason for its distrust, individual officers all say much the same things, as if they have attended the same course, or briefing. They reel off a litany of incidents in which military goodwill has been abused by unscrupulous producers and reporters. High up in their demonology is Roger Cook, whose investigative methods have left the MoD apoplectic with rage. The Army speak more in sorrow than in anger, as if they have been badly let down and will not be made fools of again.

Despite all this, we expected that ministerial permission would carry the day, but as the dates for filming drew near, we made the uncomfortable discovery that the go-ahead from the Minister meant very little. It was explained that the CO was an autocrat with the absolute right to deny access to the media on his patch. More than once in those early days the film crew would arrive at the guardroom of some regiment, only to be told, 'Sorry, lads, it's been a wasted journey. You can't come in. CO's orders.' It is always easier to say 'no' than 'yes'.

By the early summer of 1994, it looked as if there might be no series at all. But there followed a charm offensive, a series of lunches at which the production team intended to woo COs, persuading them to put aside their fears and welcome the RMP and the BBC cameras into their lives. Surely, it was argued, it would be an excellent thing for the Army to be portrayed as an open institution which solved its crimes and misdemeanours efficiently, swiftly and justly. This cut little ice with the average CO of the Blankshires (for Blankshires, read any regiment) who saw things in regimental rather than in Army terms. In fact, no COs actually attended these social gatherings. Instead, they sent their adjutants to be their ears and eyes, and the offensive ground to a halt in a haze of white wine and cocktail sausages. There *is* such a thing as a free lunch.

At the same time there were meetings at the Ministry of Defence in Whitehall with the Army's Director of Public Relations, Brig. Trousdell. The producers pleaded with him for a signed piece of paper to say that they were accredited to the Army, that the Minister approved their project, and requesting whomsoever it might concern to be as helpful as possible. This, it was hoped, might allow them past the guardroom to film the RMP about its business. The Brigadier always politely declined, offering instead to 'send a signal' to every unit the producers expected to encounter asking for its cooperation. The producers remonstrated with the brigadier quite fiercely, and a nadir in relations was reached at 'the interview without coffee'. An interview without coffee is a sign of great displeasure, and was the Army's way of saying that the producers were behaving badly. The producers certainly felt that the Army was imposing such draconian restrictions that the only explanation could be that it wanted them to abandon the project, and thus be rid of an embarrassing obligation. When facilities were suddenly withdrawn for two important and previously recced topics, it seemed almost certain that this was the case.

We had spent a lot of time in Northern Ireland pursuing an interesting and little-known RMP activity at the Complaints and Civil Courts Department in the Army Headquarters at Lisburn, outside Belfast. Under the Emergency Provisions Act, patrols have had stop-and-search powers over vehicles and people. But people also have rights – in particular, the right to lay claims against soldiers for harassment up to six years after the alleged offence. In other words, a person in Northern Ireland can say, 'A British Army patrol stopped me five years ago, and someone was rude. I am applying for compensation'. The claim has to be investigated, old patrol reports dredged up from the archives, and statements taken from the patrol leader.

It takes no great leap of the imagination to see what a time-consuming and labour-intensive process this is. The Army postings system ensures that the members of that patrol will be scattered to the four winds, and some will almost certainly have returned to civilian life. But each claim must be conscientiously investigated, and if matters come to court, soldiers have to be flown in to give evidence from wherever they are serving – Germany, Cyprus, Hong Kong, the Falkland Islands. The extremists are well aware of the potential nuisance value of the system, and they have been attempting to swamp it. One Republican sympathizer has a five-year diary involving 700 incidents. Martin McGuiness of Sinn Fein has himself filed a complaint for an incident that happened six years ago.

This is absurd. Legions of RMP personnel are employed in processing claims, tracking down witnesses, organizing their flights back, and getting them to court. The process is hugely expensive.

Even more lavish payouts occur (£5 million in 1993) as a result of low-flying aircraft, for example from Bessbrook, 'the busiest helicopter base in Europe'. Not a horse miscarries, not a sheep or cow slips a still-born lamb or calf, but it is the fault of the helicopters. Any downdraught of wind that brings a fall of soot on to (always) a brand-new carpet, was caused by the rotor blades of a helicopter. Panes of glass shatter, rickety sheds fall down – all this is the work of the same airborne foe. And so the conning goes on, supported by letters from vets, doctors and building contractors.

It was a shock, when, having prepared the programme, the Army suddenly refused all cooperation. The Chief of Staff in Northern Ireland explained that his task was to maintain peace and not provoke the community unnecessarily. By being seen to collude (sic) with the BBC in a film exposing the abuse of the complaints system, he would run the risk of jeopardizing community relations.

The second disappointment was the RMP's withdrawal of their support for the filming of the Close Protection arm of their service, the bodyguards who protect VIPs and British Embassies in sensitive areas. The reason given was that the Foreign and Commonwealth Office had vetoed the idea. But following a successful series about the FCO by the BBC, relations between the two organizations were very good, and it looked as if the FCO would not in fact raise objections to a BBC presence in a diplomatic hot-spot. It was at this point that it became clear that the real obstacle was the RMP, because it did not want its procedures made public. It is on the public record that RMP soldiers live as civilians with ambassadors and their families wherever an embassy is vulnerable (there was an RMP presence in Saigon during the Tet offensive in 1968, and has been in Beirut and in Kampala since 1980), but the RMP did not want this to be part of a high-profile television programme, and certainly did not want to show what happens when RMP soldiers become part of a diplomatic household. But it would have made a fascinating film.

So the weeks passed, and the longest days began to shorten with not a yard of videotape exposed. There was to be no Northern Ireland, no Close Protection. What was still on the agenda was General Police Duties, and the Special Investigations Branch, and yet the rules of engagement were being further refined. The Director of Public Relations decreed that on receipt of our schedule, the Army, through its own internal network, would inform all units. These units would post a set of instructions in each guardroom. Should the unit be unfortunate enough to be the target of our intentions, the order was that we should be stopped at the guardroom and the CO, his adjutant, or a duty officer summoned. That officer would then decide whether we should be admitted or shown the door. There never was a more reluctant display of enthusiasm, but this was only a beginning.

We were never on any occasion to be allowed to be on our own. We would always be accompanied by an RMP project officer 'for our own good'. This reflected the RMP's own nervousness. Aware of the general dislike of the Green Machine for the whole project, the RMP were taking no chances that we would step out of line, and do what 'the media' are perceived to do throughout the Army – falsify the facts, play tricks, bug rooms, film secretly, bite the hand that feeds it, etc., etc. A collective neurosis having seized the Army, ordinary requests were minutely analysed and misconstrued as potentially harmful. For example, an innocent request to film a general view would be turned down because there were cars in frame, and our audience of IRA bombers would write down the numbers and later blow up the cars.

By now there were two new safeguards aimed at reassuring the COs. No boards displaying the name of a regiment were to be shown. No regimental insignia on soldiers' attire to be in shot.

The other condition was that having been given permission to proceed unit by unit, the producers had to gain the unpressured permission of the soldier to be filmed. This is standard practice and there was no objection on our part. However, there was a case involving a private of the Green Howards in Catterick. He was suspected of forging MOT certificates and the RMP had arrested him. His CO agreed to allow us to film what happened 'provided the soldier himself agrees to take part'.

The soldier duly presented himself, flanked by two enormous senior NCOs, one of whom wore the red sash of the Green Howards Regimental Police. The RP spoke: 'These people', he said, 'want to film you. They are not part of us and you don't have to allow them to film. You can say no. Do you say "no"? The soldier said 'No'.

Lt. Col. Andrew Farquar of the Green Howards, the man's CO, said: 'I understand that the Royal Military Police would make a very interesting programme, but I do feel, to do it live with soldiers, when they have so many pressures, to thrust the RMP and a camera crew at him at a very stressful time . . . I think it's got to be dealt with very carefully, and I'm therefore quite pleased that that soldier has exercised a right not to have himself filmed for the programme.'

We went into this series seriously hobbled and hog-tied. The Army nearly provoked us into surrender. Looked at from a narrow regimental and career perspective, their reasons are understandable enough. We were 'the media' and we were trying to film the seamy side of the Army, so there could never be any trust. However, there is always someone somewhere prepared to make an act of faith, to take a risk, and it is to these few that we owe the series. Their names crop up throughout and without them, there would have been no series, no book.

CHAPTER 1

REPUTATIONS

They used to stand around all the London terminus stations. Always in pairs. Tall men, immaculate, webbing dazzling white, brasses glittering, creases razor-sharp, bootcaps like glass. In those days they wore weights inside their trousers where they overhung the gaiters to keep the creases vertical and to prevent rucking up. The red-topped hat had a peak at ninety degrees, which seemed to conceal the eyes entirely. Waterloo was a favourite haunt. Unless they were going south, all soldiers from Aldershot would have to stage through Waterloo. Apart from anything else, the Union Jack Club was just across the road, and they could get a cheap bed.

The Redcaps waited for their victims. We certainly felt like victims, not just because we had, many of us, to interrupt our schooling for two years to serve our country as National Servicemen, but because, having made that commitment, there was absolutely nothing to do. 'Serving our country' really did mean painting coal white. It really did mean getting down on hands and knees to pick every blade of grass from road, pavement, parade ground. It really did mean cookhouse fatigues, in which we washed chip pans coated in

A young RMP sergeant helps an old veteran at one of the fifty-year celebrations of the War.

grease in cold water without scourers or detergent. Because it filled up our time. Everyone lived for the weekend, the '36' or '48'. The former meant you could leave base at midday on Saturday and return on Sunday evening, the latter meant freedom from Friday evening – a whole two nights at home. There would have been an exodus if there had been a '12', or a '6', or even a '1', but first there was the gauntlet to run. You had to wear uniform and you were not allowed out of camp if that uniform was not immaculate.

Then there were the Redcaps at the stations, who always seemed to talk out of the corner of their mouths. Smoking a cigarette or putting hands

At a Remembrance Day parade, Royal Military Police veterans marched with the soldiers they used to police fifty years ago.

into your pockets was enough. 'Where do you think you're going, sonny?' Obsequiousness was the only defence against these bullies. They had the power, they had the stripe and how they were hated!

At the celebrations to mark the fiftieth anniversary of the Battle of Kohima, which was the turning-point in the Far Eastern campaign against the Japanese, hundreds of Second World War veterans spent a long weekend at Imphal Barracks in York and at Strensall. The Manchester Regiment, the Durham Light Infantry, some long-lost names from East Anglia, wore suits and medals, and berets with cap badges which had not been seen for many years. Their memory of the Redcaps was startlingly similar to those of the National Servicemen, and the treatment they received fifty years ago still rankles.

VETERAN 1: I was coming home on my first leave and in those days you carried everything in case you got orders to report somewhere else. Gets off at Victoria Station, Manchester and I'm loaded and this f—ing lance corporal, RMP, comes along and he says, 'Right, stand to attention. Where's your pass?' Where am I going, loaded like that? Why poor me? If I had been just coming round in a uniform, he may have a case. But I've got the lot. Rifle, pack, everything, and they pulled me. There's no need to.

VETERAN 2: Everybody knows the military police, I mean you always run away, if them bastards showed up. I mean you don't hang about, if you had any common sense . . .

VETERAN 3: Well, they had power and you had nothing. I mean it's like being a big man and you're a little man. It don't matter what you say, they will drag you in. I mean they was like the SS.

VETERAN 4: They took you in, they belted your earhole, and they took you back and that were it. No argument.

VETERAN 5: They was always looking for something, you know, that they can pick you up on. If you didn't have your gas mask, or if there was something that they could get you for, they'd get you.

VETERAN 6: They're cops, aren't they. And if you'd had a couple of beers too many, they'd pull you in, and that's it. They were doing their job, but you didn't like them. I don't think anybody did, except the guys that were in with them. They didn't mix with the ordinary guys.

VETERAN 7: They were handpicked. It was a breed of people on their own. They done their job, but they never had no mercy on ya. Whether you were right or whether you was wrong, they was always right.

VETERAN 8: I think the busiest times that they had was keeping us out of the places with the red light on them when we was on leave. Because we are that type of people. You know, everybody has to have their nuptials and that's the only place you could get 'em. This was in Bombay and Poona. They was out-of-bounds as far as the Army was concerned.

VETERAN 9: Well, they had no birth certificates!

But behind the resentment, still very much alive, there was an underlying respect, and a very British grudging fairness reflected in remarks such as 'They had a job to do, and they did it', or 'You had to have discipline in those days'. Many paid tribute to the Redcaps' traffic control, on which the convoys so often depended. While some noted the absence of Redcaps whenever the real bullets flew, one veteran generously conceded that the Redcaps bore their share of casualties.

It will always be the lot of policemen to bear the onus of hatred from those who have suffered from unjust laws. Historically the RMP have never been far from such hatred, because they have always been associated with punishment in the field. RMPs sometimes carried out the notorious 'Field Punishment Number One', or 'Crucifixion', in which a soldier is tied to an object, like a wheel, for a fixed period of time. They are particularly associated with death by firing squad, because it was the RMP who accompanied the prisoner to the place of execution where members of the soldier's own unit carried out the death penalty, and an RMP officer who delivered the *coup de grâce* on a poor wretch who, in more enlightened times, might well be tucked up in a warm psychiatric ward under therapy. The presence of the man in the red hat and the smoking revolver was noted, and it did much to blacken the RMP name, marking the Redcaps down as 'them' rather than 'us'.

There have been persistent rumours that First World War infantry soldiers who refused to 'go over the top' were shot in the trenches by the RMP. In his recent book, *The Redcaps* (1994), the military historian Dr G. D. Sheffield points out that while this practice probably occurred on a few occasions, it was unofficial, and against Army policy. Official Army policy was to publicize executions and have them witnessed by the other soldiery as a deterrent against cowardice. It is likely that those who made the original allegation would not have made a clear distinction between the RMP and the internal regimental provost NCOs, and that it was probably the latter who summarily executed soldiers for cowardice in the trenches on a few isolated occasions and not the RMP.

The uniform is traditional but Maj. Stephen Russell (left), officer commanding London District, and his RSM, WO1 G. Fox, represent a new breed of young, enthusiastic and dedicated Redcap.

What is not in doubt is that the Redcaps manned the Straggler Posts behind the front line, and picked up the dazed and bewildered soldiers, who may either genuinely have lost their way and walked away from the din of the trenches, or intended to desert. The RMP handed these men back to whatever drumhead justice the Army decided to mete out.

The RMP today would not be recognized by older ex-soldiers and the National Servicemen. It would be nice to think that this is because an enlightened Army had seen the unfairness and folly of its ways. However, it is much more to do with the fact that there is no conscription now, that this is a volunteer army, and people are simply not going to be treated any longer like dirt. It is to do with the fact that soldiers are more knowledgeable about their rights, and can no longer be insulted and assaulted with impunity. It is to do with the fact that the RMP are governed by Acts of Parliament like the Police and Criminal Evidence Act. It is more and more to do with the increasing impact of European legislation: Europe has already spoken on the treatment of pregnant servicewomen; in the future, the rights of homosexuals in the Army and the court-martial system itself are likely to come under European scrutiny.

The RMP keeps itself to itself. Where possible, Redcaps have their own bars and messes, and there is little hob-nobbing with other regiments. This makes the Redcaps seem remote and aloof even today, although a more caring, warmer image is beginning to emerge. One factor has been the increase in numbers of Redcap policewomen in and out of uniform. The Redcaps have rape crisis centres now, and they spend time counselling and supporting witnesses in difficult sex cases. We have seen an RMP patrol car give a lift to a soldier stranded out in the wilds of Lüneberg Heath, and a British soldier maced and manacled to a chair by the German police who actively welcomed the arrival of the Redcaps who had come to fetch him.

The image of the RMP embedded in people's minds after three generations of catastrophic PR and some thuggery is not suddenly going to go away, but the will and the means are there, and a start has been made.

CHAPTER 2

TRAINING

In a picturesque corner of West Sussex there is a large army barracks surrounded by high flint walls. Inside, young men and women are shouted at. This is not shouting as most of us know it, not a football match rant or a domestic wail. This is a full-scale sustained assault on the eardrums which leaves the recipient physically reeling.

If the sheer volume is not enough to cower the spirit the content surely would: 'What the shagging hell are you doing turning up at the Royal Military Police Training Centre dressed like that? Get that girlie necklace off your shagging neck, you maggot.'

This is the kind of welcome Sgt Sean O'Brien reserves for new recruits when they arrive at the training school near Chichester. He is a fearsome man, a course instructor whose task it is to mould raw young recruits into fully trained RMP corporals. He loves his job, he puts his heart and soul into it and he expects his new charges to do the same. From the moment they arrive he is a man with a mission: living, eating and drinking the business of imparting the corps message to his new squad.

Like a preacher before a congregation the good sergeant holds forth on the corps, its history, functions and ideals: '*Exemplo Ducemus*' – by example shall we lead. This is the corps motto; it is also something you will live by. We

Dawn: recruits' accomodation block. Lights on at 6 am.

police the army, and in order to do that effectively we have to earn their respect. We cannot achieve that if we are found wanting in our behaviour, attitude, ability, or dress. The RMP must be "beyond reproach" at all times. If you don't think you can live up to these standards, go now, we don't want you. If you stay and fall below them we will throw you out anyway.'

One of Sgt O'Brien's favourite missives is Training Objective 401. TO401 is a declaration of RMP standards, a long list of virtues and morals which would make a saint

*Sgt O'Brien faced with a
new recruit wearing jeans.*

think twice before signing up. It is also Sgt O'Brien's reason for living. On one occasion he was furious with one of the recruits, not for the minor misdemeanour he had committed but for telling a white lie when quizzed. 'TO401, honesty at all times. I don't expect you to be perfect but I do expect you to be honest. TO401 – got it!' The pale recruit nodded and as far as we know never told an untruth again.

During our first week of filming, two new recruits left within days of arriving, while the rest wavered under the intense pressure of living up to Sgt O'Brien's 'standards': 'We put them through it the first two weeks. It's a good way of weeding out the weak – not just physically, but mentally as well. You can't send the timid out to face thirty drunken squaddies on a Saturday night. They have got to be able to take the crap and cope. Those that fall by the wayside are the ones who would freeze in a real situation. When that happens people get hurt. By weeding them out now we save them from ever having to face a situation with which they could not cope.'

As the new course progressed we realized that there was a reason for everything that the good sergeant did. What at first appeared to be gratuitous bollockings began to make sense as we learned the grand purpose behind it all. The harsh welcome was designed to shock the new recruits into 'putting their military heads back on'. It worked very well.

The sustained attack on standards had the effect of making the recruits realize that to fail or give up meant an admission of 'personal low standards'. No one wants to admit that *they* do not have high standards. It also gave them an intense pride in being part of an organization that expects and gets the best from its members.

The haranguing drew the squad together as they closed ranks to face the common enemy – the nasty sergeant: 'All good team-building techniques. What I look for is people starting to help each other. I give recruit A a ticking off for dirty boots or poor turn-out and pretty soon recruits B and C are pitching in and helping him get his kit sorted out so that the nasty sergeant doesn't pick on him again. In no time at all they are starting to work as a unit.'

Other techniques include the fostering of unit pride. There are always two courses running side by side, Sgt O'Brien's 9420 Alpha and Sgt Brown's 9420 Bravo. Sgt O'Brien always referred to the Bravo squad as the 'Maggot squad'. This was done in public, whenever the other squad marched past: 'Eyes right, maggot squad approaching.' His new recruits loved it and quickly expended extra effort to try and beat 'the maggots' at everything.

The next thing that happened surprised us a great deal. Sgt O'Brien was ticked off by the company sergeant major in front of his squad for the poor turn-out of some of the recruits. They were open-mouthed as the man who had done nothing but shout and bawl at them was suddenly on the receiving end of a similar tirade.

Afterwards, we discovered the reason. 'The CSM sees something amiss and gives me an ear-bending. The recruits realize that I am getting it because they fell down on standards, they feel guilty, they have let me down – result, next time they try harder.'

The recruits responded as he had hoped: 'Sgt O'Brien may be a **** to work for but he is fair. You put one hundred per cent in and he will back you all the way. When he got bollocked by the CSM it really wasn't his fault.'

Building that personal loyalty is the hallmark of any good instructor. Sgt O'Brien was very good at it, and he succeeded because he genuinely cared for his recruits. He put a huge amount of time and effort into training them and they responded by doing the very best they could for him. The change that took place in some of the recruits was quite extraordinary. From the very beginning he made each recruit stand up in front of the others and tell his life story. For some it was a breeze, for others a real nightmare. The shy among them were given encouragement but still made to perform. 'It's all about confidence. They have got to be able to be confident enough to command respect, they will have to stand up in front of people and take command of a situation. You can't do that if you are a shrinking violet.'

As time passed, the violets gradually blossomed until they were more than happy to take their turn in one of Sgt O'Brien's enforced joke-telling sessions: 'Tell me a joke, Baxter' – 'Bill and Ben the flowerpot men in bed: Bill says, "lobba lobba lob"; Ben says - "You'll swallow it if you love me." ' Sgt O'Brien shook his head sadly.

Humour is one of the tools Sgt O'Brien uses to get his recruits to respond in the right way. It is a way of letting off steam and encouraging team spirit. During one locker inspection one of the recruits was accused of being a 'train spotter' because he had an anorak among his civilian clothes. At the next inspection the locker door sported a picture of a train. It was not missed by Sgt O'Brien who instantly recognized it for what it was – a subtle and humorous up-yours from the recruit. Sgt O'Brien began a lengthy and detailed discussion with the recruit on the interests and merits of being a train spotter.

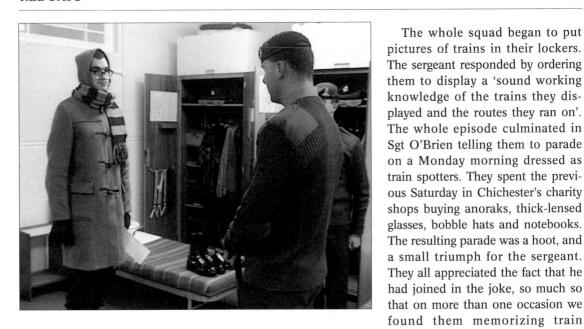

Train-spotter inspection.

The whole squad began to put pictures of trains in their lockers. The sergeant responded by ordering them to display a 'sound working knowledge of the trains they displayed and the routes they ran on'. The whole episode culminated in Sgt O'Brien telling them to parade on a Monday morning dressed as train spotters. They spent the previous Saturday in Chichester's charity shops buying anoraks, thick-lensed glasses, bobble hats and notebooks. The resulting parade was a hoot, and a small triumph for the sergeant. They all appreciated the fact that he had joined in the joke, so much so that on more than one occasion we found them memorizing train timetables and locomotive types.

Slogans like 'Positive attitude', 'Healthy body, healthy mind' and even 'Shiny boots, shiny mind' were used daily until even the film crew started to worry about the state of the shine on their shoes. At times like these the whole place had a palpable 1950s feel to it. The pervading ethos was so positive and wholesome that we felt as if we were taking part in one of those old government information films where scores of enthusiastic youths in white baggy shorts perform callisthenics.

Certainly the corps' moral standards are very much rooted in a bygone age. There cannot be many organizations nowadays where an instructor would be in serious jeopardy of losing his job simply for becoming a little too friendly with a pupil. In the corps this is regarded as a very serious problem, as is any hint of sexual impropriety between ranks. If a senior officer uses his rank to press his attentions upon a junior rank, his chances of avoiding disgrace if discovered are nil.

The corps' moral code is so completely black and white that in the 1990s, when these issues are at best extremely grey, they seem a welcome and refreshingly simple blast from the past. If something is wrong it is wrong, simple as that. If you transgress you are punished, no appeal, you tow the line or you go.

The recruits seemed to be relieved that the regime was so strict and unbending. For many of them this was the first time anyone had suggested to them that they should strive for anything better than the minimum. For some it was a release from the complex and conflicting world in which they had grown up. In a way, Sgt O'Brien was the father they never had: strict, fair, encouraging and fun.

If pressed, army folk will wax lyrical about their achievements, the skills they have learned, the courses they have completed, how they have progressed. Their lives are similar to a train on a railway track: you can go forwards as slowly or as fast as you like, but it is very difficult to fall off. For the rest of us who live without such reassuring parameters, life is never that straight and simple.

For the new recruits at Chichester this new life of hard-and-fast rules, shouting sergeants and even more terrifying CSMs was something they quickly learned to love. When we asked them after a particularly unpleasant day whether they wanted to give up and go home, they said, 'No way. It may be bloody awful now but on the whole it's great. You know as long as you do what they want and stick to the rules it's all right. Besides, where else could you have such a laugh with no worries?'

It was the women who seemed to enjoy the whole experience the most. They had a much more pragmatic attitude to the shouting and privations and did not take it as seriously as the boys. On a number of occasions we found them falling about in hysterics over a bollocking or a mistake. They did not take it personally and seemed better at understanding the 'hidden agenda'.

The RMP have a surprisingly high proportion of women in their ranks.

Young RMP recruits doing the 'Log Run', a test of character and endurance.

Although on occasions RMP corporals are required to physically restrain violent soldiers, women are still well represented in the corps. They serve alongside their male counterparts and face their share of the trouble. As one experienced sergeant explained, a drunken soldier will often have no qualms about attacking another man even if he is wearing an RMP uniform. However, that same soldier, presented with a woman, will often think twice about it. It seems that the armed forces have been particularly successful in instilling a proper respect towards women into their young soldiers. Often the only person who can diffuse a violent situation or persuade a dangerous man to give himself up is a woman.

That is not to say the women of the RMP do not experience their share of violence; they do. There are numerous stories of women breaking up fights and giving as good as they get. During their training at Chichester women are offered no favours. They do exactly the same things as the men. This can be a bit of a shock for girls who have been taught non-violence all their lives. They can find themselves being exhorted to 'tighten that arm-lock till it hurts'. A soldier in pain is a disabled soldier and one that cannot hit you.

The same applies in the small arms weapon training. The RMP all carry a weapon. The fact is they very rarely ever draw weapons, let alone fire them, but they must all be competent in their use. This means an intensive small arms course and a comprehensive test. During the course, range work is very important and here the men and women will be taught weapon safety, how to handle a gun, fire it and maintain it.

One of the things some of them seem to find hardest to learn is the possibility that one day they may actually have to shoot another person. They were expertly drilled and they dutifully made the right replies when questioned about the circumstances in which they would be justified in using a weapon. But afterwards many confided that if push came to shove, unless a life was in danger, they would not fire. It is not a matter of cowardice but more a desire not to inflict unnecessary pain or suffering.

Unnecessary pain and suffering certainly will be part of the job if these soldiers pass out of Chichester. The RMP have a child abuse unit which deals with all suspected cases of abuse within army families. It was set up by a woman warrant officer but is run both by RMP women and men. They spend a large part of their time counselling and working with the parents.

Their work starts with a complaint or phone call telling them that a particular child may be at risk. They then hold a case conference to decide whether intervention is needed. If it is, they visit the child's home and talk to everyone concerned. If it seems serious, they will arrange an informal interview with the child.

They have a special flat where a great deal of care has been taken to make the surroundings 'comfortable and reassuring'. There are also two video cameras to tape interviews. The cameras are set on wide and close-up. The close-up one records tell-tale gestures and expressions, occasionally an indication that a child is anxious and hiding something. The wide-angle camera records the movements of the children's arms and hands as they re-enact events and point to different parts of their anatomy.

In cases of suspected sexual abuse a set of dolls is used. These have the correct anatomy for male and female so a child can point to an area where they might have been touched. The dolls consist of mother, father, brother and sister. Surprisingly, a large proportion of sexual abuse takes place between brothers and sisters, with the older child abusing a younger one.

The unit also deals with rape victims where a sympathetic ear and non-threatening surroundings are needed to help the victim recount her ordeal. The women who are involved in the unit are passionate about its worth and put a great deal of effort into caring for their young charges.

To prepare the women for all of this, the Training Centre at Chichester has its own share of women instructors. They run the same courses as the men and take new batches of recruits through their paces in the same way. In fact, some say that the female instructors are stricter and harder to please than their male colleagues.

Either way, they all genuinely seem to care about their recruits and want them to be a credit to the corps. As Sgt O'Brien explained, 'If you want to lead by example you have to be "beyond reproach", and to do that you have to be the best.'

CAPT. FRANCES WEST

Frances West was good news. The camera crew will not hear an ill-word spoken of her. They had just flown into Croatia. On the next day they would drive up over the mountains to the British headquarters in Vitez in Bosnia.

It had been an ill-omened trip. In off-loading the camera gear from the carousel at the little airport at the Croatian town of Split on the Dalmatian coast, the crew had taken off what they assumed was the director's bag. It was only when they got to the hotel that the awful discovery was made, that what they had taken was an identical bag to his, full of female attire, mostly black. So it was no surprise — for it had been that sort of day — when the crew left the restaurant, where they had been socializing with Capt. Frances West and some other officers, to find that their hire-car had been stolen. At this point, all the male officers seemed to disappear, but not Frances West. She stopped, she thought, she said, 'I've got a hunch', and then she strode purposefully across the square.

She was on her way to the local police station, where, through an interpreter, she explained the difficulty. She asked if she could look for the car in the pound at the back, and there it was. The police demanded a large fine for illegal parking before they would release it, although it had been legally parked. On the way back, Frances West explained that she had overheard a snatch of conversation the previous week in which someone said that the Croatian police were so hard up that they had taken to this means of bolstering police funds — an admirable piece of sleuthing!

Capt. Frances West is the top British military policeperson in one of the Army's toughest postings. She commands thirty-four Redcaps, mostly men. She polices 3,500 British troops and her patch extends from HQ in balmy Split up into the Bosnian hinterland of ravaged Gornji Vakuf, Tomislavgrad and Vitez.

Here, on operational duty, crime is not high on the RMP agenda. Neither officers nor men are allowed more than two cans of beer in a twenty-four-hour period, and as there is no intoxication, there is very little misbehaviour. The type of policing is completely different. In February 1994, after the most vicious blood-letting, a fragile peace broke out between Croat and Muslim, an alliance of convenience against a common enemy – the Serbs. Evidence of the brutality that neighbour showed neighbour is all around. The whiff of ethnic cleansing hangs heavy in the air.

The role of the Redcaps is quasi-diplomatic. The day may begin with obligatory slivovitz toasting with the local constabulary. Then sergeants and corporals in a white painted UN Landrover will carry out joint police patrols with Croatians and Muslims, or sometimes both. They visit checkpoints that straddle the old battle lines, where the two sides still gaze sullenly across a no-man's-land. 'Policemen talk to other policemen,' says Capt. West. 'By trying to get the Muslims and Croats out on the road patrolling together, (the RMP hope) they'll actually start talking to one another, and realize perhaps that they have a lot in common.' One promising sign of détente was that Frances West and her men felt safe enough to wear blue berets instead of blue helmets.

It is easy to be cynical, to question how some intelligent young Brits in blue berets and red RMP brassards are going to mediate away a mutual hatred that goes back centuries. Easy too to put down the local enthusiasm for joint patrolling to the fact that they get a free tank of petrol in a country where petrol hardly exists outside military sources. It is still impressive to see Capt. West and her men going about their business in the unshakeable belief that they are contributing to the peace process. As the tortuous truces crash about their ears, their optimism is touching.

In Bosnia, Capt. West carries a pistol and a rifle and ammunition. 'I would shoot', she says, 'if I felt within the rules of engagement that my life was threatened. I would hope that my training would take over and I would use it effectively.' Her eyes have a steely glint at this point, and one wonders why the Ministry of Defence still refuses to let women be infantry soldiers or drive tanks.

Like many Redcaps, Frances West has a service background. Her father was an RMP staff sergeant, but she did not set out to join the Army. After schooling in Folkestone and Colchester, she went into accounting, auxiliary night nursing, and was the London manager of the Royal National Institute for the Blind, before martial stirrings prompted an application to Sandhurst, which she left as a lieutenant at the age of twenty-four.

Frances West has done everything right from an Army point of view. She is in the right job and the right rank at the right age. She enjoys the work. She can naturally expect her career to move smoothly upwards to major and beyond. But she is not married. What if she were? What if she were to have a family? The Army has learned by bitter experience in the courts that it cannot discharge pregnant servicewomen. Capt. Frances West says, 'I would like to get married and possibly have a family in the future, but I think it would be very difficult to combine motherhood with the job I do. If you're earning the sort of salary that I'm earning [in 1995 an Army captain gets between £21,794 and £25,331 p.a.] it would be quite easy to arrange professional childcare on an eight to six basis. But my job isn't eight to six. I'm here for six months. If I had a couple of children, who would be looking after them?'

Capt. West took us in convoy through parts of central Bosnia that made us want to look away. Man's inhumanity to man was all around. Between cheerful Alpine-style chalet homes, with piles of logs neatly cut ready for winter and children gambolling in the garden, were blackened roofless homes in overgrown gardens. These people had been neighbours. Capt. West got our little hire-car refuelled at military petrol dumps and she always saw that we were looked after on military bases. You could tell that the men she commanded liked and respected her. She in turn brought a feminine sensitivity to her command role. A smile, a softness, an awareness that must never be misinterpreted as weakness, but which a male counterpart is totally incapable of imparting.

Having landed such a high-profile job so young, Capt. West may already have reached a climax in her career. At least, when the conflict is over, she may return to relive the 'time of her life'. 'It's one of the most beautiful countries I have ever been to in my entire life,' she says. 'I would love to come back here for a holiday. The scenery just takes your breath away.' (Frances West was subsequently promoted to major in the summer of 1995.)

CHAPTER 3

ON THE STREETS

The majority of RMP personnel are corporals; they are the men and women on the streets. They patrol Army establishments and garrison towns twenty-four hours a day, seven days a week, all year round. In Army-speak they are 'the front-line troops'. In civilian-speak they are 'the poor sods who do all the work'.

Patrolling is the largest part of their daily work. For the vast majority of the time it is mind-numbingly tedious. Patrols have certain patches they have to cover, making a designated number of appearances in various 'hot-spots' each night. This means hours of cruising around in a conspicuous car under the watchful and suspicious gaze of every soldier they pass. Occasionally, the scene has an almost balletic feel to it: the patrol car cruises 'shark-like' into an area full of potential customers or 'minnows'. As soon as it appears they flit away, arguments cease and all is sweetness and light. When it is gone, the revelry continues undisturbed.

The patrols seem content to chase shadows: 'Our mere presence is a big deterrent factor for most squaddies.' Although this is certainly true, it makes their job a difficult combination of inaction for long periods of time, with sudden high levels of stress and great personal danger. When trouble does start someone usually gets the 'good news' – not a free trip to Disneyland or a win on the pools but an Army description of someone who has been severely assaulted. Getting the 'good news' seems to happen to someone on a fairly regular basis in most large Army establishments.

In Germany, in the small town of Bergen close to a large garrison, the 'good news' is received monthly. At the end of the month the soldiers are paid, and the following weekend most single, bored soldiers gravitate to Bergen where wine, women and song are in plentiful supply. The alcohol is usually consumed in the cheap NAAFI bars on camp before being topped up with strong German beer in Bergen's bars later in the evening. The women, mostly German, seem to come from far and wide to meet solvent, exciting British soldiers for an evening of fun. The 'song' is supplied by the Time Euro Disco which is a large establishment designed to meet the needs of British soldiers on the town. The fact that trouble of some kind often erupts is no surprise to the young men of the RMP: 'We expect something to happen at some point over the weekend, we just never know when or where.'

During one of our filming weekends we were sitting outside the disco,

Opposite: 'To police the Army effectively, we must earn their respect. To do that, we must be beyond reproach.'

Redcaps wait for trouble outside the Time Euro Disco in Bergen, Germany.

watching the comings and goings with a patrol and the RMP dog-handler. There seemed to be a notice-able number of people wandering off to the banks of a nearby lake and then returning some time later. When quizzed the corporals explained that this was the place couples went for sex when there were no other conve-nient places available. It appeared that girls who had travelled some distance to the disco had no local accommodation for the purpose, so the banks of the lake were an attractive solution to the problem.

Armed with this enticing piece of information, we were delighted when someone reported a disturbance at the lake. The corporals summoned the help of the dog-handler, produced powerful torches and headed off into Cupid's corridor.

We had not gone far when we were met by the sight of a black soldier, naked to the waist and flanked by a girl and another man. Not surprisingly, they were a little shocked to see the RMP, a lot of light, a snarling dog and a film crew. There followed what can only be described as a nasty altercation. The young black soldier became upset at the presence of the camera, threat-ened to sue everyone within earshot and loudly proclaimed that he was being victimized because of his colour. The fact that the RMP suspected him of being involved in a disturbance and that he appeared to be covered in some kind of body oil did not trouble him a bit.

What did get his attention though was Lucifer the dog. The girl made a sudden movement towards his handler and in the time it takes to say 'ouch' nearly became an appetizer for the big German shepherd. The dog was restrained as the girl beat a hasty retreat, loud snarls ringing in her ears. She had been very lucky. A few years earlier, one of Lucifer's predecessors had been confronted by a 'hard' squaddie who jabbed his finger at the dog as he shouted he was not 'scared of any f——ing dog'.

Unfortunately for him the dog was not scared of any f——ing soldier either and promptly bit off the end of his finger. As for Lucifer, he had but one sim-ple desire in life: he wanted to bite someone. He was not fussy – soldiers, civilians, RMP, BBC film crews, it was all the same to him. He just wanted to sink those large, straight, beautiful white teeth into someone, anybody, rather than spend his time sitting in the back of his handler's Landrover.

At the lakeside he had been denied yet again and he was a very cross dog. In addition to his barking and whining to be let loose to do what he does best, our continued presence with the camera was beginning to make our cor-poral's life almost impossible. We made a tactical withdrawal leaving our long-suffering project officer trying to calm the irate soldier and reassure him that his shining torso would not appear on national prime-time television, which may have been a big mistake since, if it had, he may have had all sorts

HIGH SPIRITS

In Germany, the RMP police a large contingent of the British Army. Although most of their work is straightforward and fairly routine, occasionally something happens which can make a long night shift a real joy.

One such occasion involved a group of officers from a much respected regiment based in Fallingbostl. On this particular night, the officers were celebrating the arrival of a new brother officer and the departure of another. The party went on for some time until all concerned were very much the worse for drink. In the Army, where officers are concerned, this is known as 'high spirits' – enlisted men get drunk, officers get 'high-spirited'.

These 'high-spirited' officers decided to welcome the new recruit into the fold by playing a prank on him. After some discussion they decided that the best wheeze would be to set a booby-trap in the new incumbent's bedroom. This involved placing a thunder flash in a metal wastepaper basket and then filling it with flour. The idea was that, when detonated, the explosive charge would throw up a huge cloud of flour to cover the room and the unsuspecting officer. The device was primed and the officers eagerly awaited the return of their victim. When he arrived it was detonated.

As the thunder flash ignited it threw the flour up into the air as intended, but a split second later reached the right density to instantaneously combust. The result was a colossal explosion. The man closest to the bin was quite severely hurt, others nearby were also badly hurt.

The building was partly demolished. Those left on their feet realized that the injured had to be given medical attention immediately, so a car was commandeered and the injured were bundled in before setting off for the garrison medical centre.

So far things had gone badly wrong for the pranksters, but unfortunately for them they were just about to get worse. The erratic progress of the car brought its inebriated occupants to the attention of an RMP patrol. They stopped the car and found it to contain a lot of drunk and injured officers covered in flour. The driver was breathalysed.

Medical treatment was given and the officers responsible were duly charged with reckless behaviour and causing criminal damage to Army property, something for which three of them were fined £3,000 each, whilst the driver was prosecuted for drunk-driving.

During the investigation that followed it was discovered that the damaged building used to be part of Hitler's hunting lodge during the Second World War and that the Allies had tried very hard to destroy it. If only Churchill had known he could have saved himself a great deal of trouble. He could simply have sent a bunch of 'high-spirited' officers over with a wastepaper bin, a thunder flash, and a packet of flour.

of offers, perhaps even some for an alternative career.

When the corporals are not dealing with young soldiers with a penchant for baby oil, they spend a great deal of time dealing with young soldiers with a penchant for large quantities of drink. When filming in Hohne in northern Germany during the hot summer of 1994, we often witnessed the problems and abuse that the corporals are subjected to when the British soldier has had 'one over the eight'. On one occasion a patrol stopped a group of soldiers as they walked back to their barracks after a night of drinking in the town. The corporals had spent a good part of the evening trying to discover who had been dismantling and destroying road signs in the area. They suspected the noisy group heading back to camp were the culprits.

As they approached, the atmosphere changed dramatically. Gone was the banter and singing, replaced by 'Here come the Bastards' (the squaddies' nickname for the RMP) and a lot of low, mumbled threats. The film crew observed from a distance as the corporals started to question the soldiers.

Almost immediately they started to shout abuse at the corporals, denying any wrongdoing. We were surprised by this disregard for the authority of the RMP until it became obvious that the reason behind it was quite simply a matter of numbers. The soldiers were in the majority, they were drunk and felt confident as they backed each other up. The two corporals were facing a situation which threatened to become violent very quickly unless they did something. They either had to back down or take control before things got out of hand.

We had quickly reached that stage in a confrontation which some people have described as 'time standing still' – the moment before an explosion when everyone is suddenly aware that something is about to happen. Into this moment stepped the more experienced of the two corporals. He looked hard at the ringleader of the group and spoke in a very quiet voice. It was almost a whisper and, although we were too far away to hear what was said, the effect was almost instantaneous. The soldiers seemed to be shocked, there was a collective blink before they stepped back, mumbled disconsolately and shuffled off back to camp. We did not ask what had been said – it probably was not repeatable anyway – the corporal just smiled when he returned to the car, and we went on our way.

Unfortunately for the RMP, it is not always that easy to maintain their authority. During the same week, we were present when a patrol had stopped what appeared to be an overloaded car full of drunk soldiers' wives. They had just been to a 'women only' evening where they had watched a Chippendale-type group strut their stuff. This car-load of extremely happy young girls were delighted to be stopped by a couple of handsome chaps in shiny, smart uniforms. The comments that floated out of the car made one corporal's neck turn as red as his cap. If this was not enough to ruin his day, a group of merry squaddies who were standing nearby at a taxi rank struck up with the theme tune from the American 1960s comedy series 'The Monkees'. 'The Monkeys' is one of the other nicknames the RMP enjoy. The corporal gamely continued to check the driver's details while he was serenaded with quite a tuneful rendition in one ear and a licentious proposition in the other. We made a tactical withdrawal and left him to his tormentors.

Although the soldiers are quick to ridicule or abuse the RMP there are quite a few occasions when they need them and are more than glad to see the arrival of those red caps. During our filming in Osnabrück to the south we were on patrol with a pair of corporals when they received a call to attend the local German police station where a British soldier was being held. The patrol headed for the station while the film crew reflected on something we had learned a few days earlier: if you are a soldier based in Germany you may find that you live under a different set of rules from the rest of the population.

Soldiers and RMP corporals had explained that, in any German town where there was a large concentration of British troops, the local police usually had a reputation for action first and questions later. This may not be surprising since the British soldier in Germany does not have a blameless reputation, but the speed with which the German police are reported to use force when dealing with British servicemen does cause some concern.

When our corporals arrived at the police station the fact that they were trailing a BBC film crew caused a certain amount of confusion. After a few minutes' discussion with our interpreter we were allowed to follow the corporals through to the interview room where the soldier was being held. He sat on a plastic chair, head bowed. Opposite him sat a German policeman at a desk working away at a typewriter, compiling a report. Our soldier was handcuffed and dishevelled, but the most striking thing about him was his eyes. They were red, very swollen, and watering continuously. He looked as though he had gone ten rounds with Mike Tyson in a bad mood.

When the RMP corporal asked him what had happened, he had to be reassured that the policeman opposite did not speak English before he would begin. He had apparently arranged to meet some other soldiers from his unit in one of the town's discos. When he arrived he could not find them so he had a few drinks. Having consumed a fair amount of drink, he left. On the walk back to his barracks he discovered an abandoned bicycle, and decided he would take it. As soon as he mounted it he discovered the reason it had been abandoned – it had a flat tyre. At this point the German police 'appeared from nowhere' and asked him if he was the owner of the bike. He admitted he was not. He was a little vague about what happened next but claimed he was attacked by the German police and that it was unprovoked.

Our corporal suspected the truth lay nearer the fact that he might have been 'a little mouthy' when he should not have. Whatever the reason, the result was the use of force by the arresting police. He had been sprayed in the face with CS gas at very close range before being forced over the bonnet of a car and handcuffed. Although this explained his poor state, it did not explain the sanguine attitude he displayed towards the treatment he had just received. When questioned, it appeared he thought this was the natural outcome of any contact with the German police. In the meantime, our corporals negotiated his release so he could be returned to the care of the Army.

The RMP have to maintain a good working relationship with the German civil police. They often work together, especially if a British soldier has committed an offence against a German civilian. Consequently, the higher ranks in the corps will not make any comments about the way the German police do their job. However, the lower ranks will offer an opinion if pushed; they consider that the German Civil Police or 'GCP', have a surprising amount of leeway when it comes to dealing with British servicemen, something the RMP would not have if the situation was reversed. As one corporal observed, 'They haven't quite got the hang of community policing over here yet.'

Eventually our patrol was allowed to take the soldier away and they duly returned him to his unit. There he was met by an officer who was very annoyed with him, not for getting into trouble with the German police but for dragging a BBC film crew back with him. He was extremely concerned about the image of the regiment and was terrified that they would be portrayed on national television as a unit of bicycle thieves. The next day the soldier was hauled up in front of his CO and fined £100 for being drunk. We never found out what happened to the bike.

When the RMP are not actually out on the streets dealing with incidents as they happen, they often find themselves having to pick up the pieces after crimes have been committed. In Honhe we filmed the aftermath of a particularly nasty fight which had occurred in a bar on the garrison camp just 200 yards from the RMP police station.

The perpetrators of the fight would have probably got clean away with it had it not been for the eagle eye and quick reactions of the sergeant on duty that night. He was at his desk when he received a call from The Oak (a pub on camp) that there had been a fight. From his vantage-point at the front desk, he saw a small group of men leaving camp in a hurry. He rushed out of the station and confronted them. There followed a great deal of shouting, the young men were determined to leave, and they were not going to be stopped by anyone. Without laying a finger on them and by his sheer personal presence the sergeant kept the men rooted to the spot despite a great deal of abuse and provocation. Reinforcements arrived and the young men were detained. Had he not done this they would have probably left the camp and got away with an attack which had left two people seriously injured and one disfigured for life.

Of all the things we saw while researching and filming the series, this incident was the one thing that brought home to us the high quality and calibre of the people that make up the RMP. Indeed, the sergeant's actions perfectly encapsulated the corps motto – *Exemplo Ducemus*. The sergeant handled a very difficult job with tact, efficiency and firmness. The outcome was never in any doubt – those young men were not going to leave and that was that.

The whole sorry business had started much earlier in the evening when Cpl Horne of Hohne Barracks had decided to take his Scandinavian wife for a quiet drink to celebrate their first year of marriage. They went to The Oak, which is a NAAFI-run pub on camp and as such is subsidized by the Army. Because of this, the pub is very popular with the soldiers, as well as with any-one else who manages to get on camp to take advantage of the cheap beer.

Security on the main gate at this time was not particularly strict with regards to who should and who should not be allowed in. Consequently, when four young men approached the checkpoint and only one of them was authorized to enter, all four were allowed on camp. Had the security been as it should, the events that followed would never have happened.

The young men headed straight for The Oak and the cheap beer, and ended up sitting on the table next to Cpl Horne. By now, the Cpl and his wife had been joined by two friends and the four of them talked for some time. At one point during the evening Cpl Horne's wife was drawn into conversation with the young men. This conversation was not an entirely friendly one it seems, and drew to a close as Cpl Horne and his party decided to leave. At this point it seems the young men insulted Cpl Horne's wife. There followed a brief exchange between the corporal and the men after which Cpl Horne left with his friends and wife.

At that moment, all hell broke loose. Witnesses reported that Cpl Horne and his friends were attacked from behind by the young men with broken bottles and beer glasses. Whatever the precise details of who was attacked first and by whom, the result was never in dispute. Bdr Griffith, one of Cpl Horne's friends, was struck to the ground where he was repeatedly and viciously kicked. He sustained severe bruising and a badly damaged neck. The other friend, Colin Miles, tried to pull the attackers away and was hit over the head from behind with what was probably a bottle. He was struck twice before falling to the floor.

Cpl Horne was the most severely injured. He was struck from behind with a broken glass to the face. The injuries he received suggest that he was glassed twice since he had so many deep cuts that it was difficult to see how one strike could have caused so much damage. His face was sliced right through to the inside of his mouth, he was cut repeatedly about the mouth and lips and ended up having to hold the front of his mouth together. He was extremely lucky that they missed his eyes.

To say the attack was horrific would be a fair description of what took place. What is more difficult to put across on the small screen or on a page is the sheer base vileness of someone who attacks a man from behind with a weapon and without warning with the express intention of causing serious harm.

The brave young men that did this then left their victims literally in pools of blood and attempted to walk out of camp. Had it not been for the presence of the RMP, they would almost certainly have walked free. Instead they were caught and detained while the corporals on the ground began the difficult task of finding out who was responsible.

At that time we were in the RMP police station on camp. When the sergeant rushed out to stop the young men leaving we followed and filmed the story as it progressed. It became clear that the RMP had a very difficult task on their hands. It appeared that the four men were made up of two sets of brothers. One set were the sons of the garrison secondary school headmaster; the other two were entirely unconnected with the military. The RMP only have jurisdiction over 'dependants' – Army employees and their 'dependant' families. Consequently, they could only arrest the headmaster's sons if they could establish that the boys were living with their parents and so could be classed as dependant. While the Special Investigation Branch desperately tried to sort that out, the corporals on the ground were busy at the garrison medical centre coping with the injured. Doctors were called from their beds to tend to the worst cases while the corporals began to take initial statements from the victims and witnesses.

It quickly became clear that the attackers were mixed in with the victims in the operating-room. One of them had a severe cut to one of his hands and his three friends had been brought to the medical centre by the RMP as a temporary holding measure.

The net result of this unhappy situation was that Cpl Horne found himself sitting on a bench holding his face on and watching a doctor sew one of his attackers' wrists back together. The situation further deteriorated when the other young men started laughing at the distress of Cpl Horne's wife. The whole scene had a nightmare *Clockwork Orange* feel about it.

In the midst of all this misery, the medical centre doctors and nurses continued to patch, clean and comfort. The RMP tried to impose some kind of order and we stood and filmed in utter astonishment. They displayed a sort of calm 'business as usual' professionalism as they went about their separate tasks and this made one realize that this was the norm – soldiers and civilians bleeding all over the place was just another day for the RMP and the medics.

When it was all over and the blood had been mopped up, the RMP still had a difficult job on their hands. Statements had to be taken, reports written up and the whole lot put together so that some form of prosecution could be brought against the attackers. In the end, the difficulties over jurisdiction meant the RMP could not pursue the case themselves. However, they were able to provide enough evidence for Cpl Horne to continue a civil case against the four young men. Had the RMP not acted so quickly, there would have been no evidence available and no chance of bringing the young men to court.

If you are a new young lance corporal fresh out of training and posted to Germany, you are very likely to attend at least one fatal road traffic accident in your first year. The RMP attend all accidents that involve service personnel. In 1994 the RMP investigated over 4,500 motoring offences. Half that total were traffic accidents and sixty of those were fatal. In the Hohne region of Germany where there is a large concentration of troops, fatal RTAs happen about once a month.

The area is flat and wide, the roads straight and fast with unforgiving corners every couple of kilometres. Most of the young unattached soldiers have a high disposable income, food and accommodation are provided, and this often leaves in excess of £600 a month to spend as they please. Cars are relatively

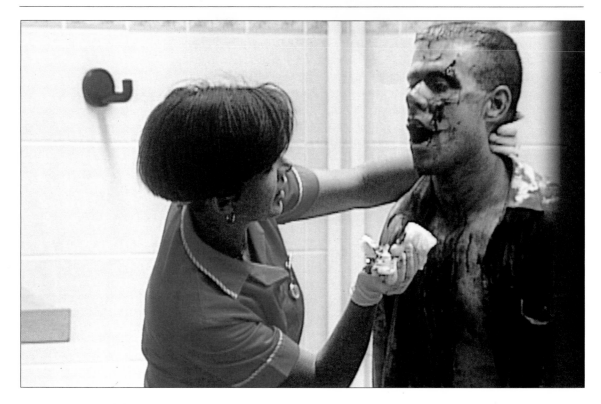

A nurse tries to stem the flow of blood caused by a broken glass to the face of Cpl Horne.

cheap, and there are favourable discounts for servicemen. The cars can be driven to the UK after a year and sold for the original purchase price. One has only to look at the vehicles parked outside most Army accommodation blocks to realize that the average British soldier in Germany is doing very well.

As well as a good financial deal, the soldier has a wide range of powerful cars to choose from. Most of the younger soldiers go for fast cars, and, come pay-day, with money in his pocket and the wide open roads beckoning, many take off for a weekend away from camp. They may go as far as Amsterdam, only a few hours' drive on the autobahn, or they may stay locally and tour the nightspots. Either way, it is not surprising that on some Friday and Saturday nights the RMP duty room in Hohne should be called out to a traffic accident.

Just before our filming in August 1994, we were told of a young soldier who had misjudged a bend and lost control of his car. He had died a horrible death, trapped in a burning wreck before help could reach him. The corporals who attend these accidents are usually the same age as the victims they try to help. They are remarkably matter-of-fact about it all: 'When you get to a really bad one you just have to concentrate on the job and try to ignore the mess. You cannot let your feelings show. With everyone else running around screaming and shouting, if you lost your cool as well it would be a disaster.'

We attended only one such accident. We were doing the graveyard shift, from midnight to seven in the morning, when our patrol was called to go to an accident which involved two servicemen's wives somewhere out in the countryside. It was five in the morning and a new day was just beginning to lift the landscape up out of the shadows.

Despite their tiredness, our corporals set off at great speed to attend the accident and its victims. When we arrived we found two young women standing at the side of a long narrow road. Their car had a large dent in the front and they looked shocked and miserable. We assumed the worst and looked down the road for signs of the victim.

He was about 450 ft back up the road and quite dead. The younger of the two corporals went to take a closer look before reporting back to the group by the car: 'Oh dear, oh dear, that is definitely one dead deer.'

There was an embarrassed silence whilst we the film crew adjusted our perceptions of the situation, and the driver smiled weakly at the corporal's joke. The women had been travelling fairly fast along the road and the light was just beginning to break when a deer had run across the road. They had no chance of avoiding it and now they were stuck with a damaged car, a dead deer and an RMP patrol for company.

We left the corporals taking statements and filling out forms. For them, their night shift would have the worst possible end, a time-consuming accident to sort out, and a case to write up once they got back to the duty room. Patrols are expected to complete their reports before they leave the station. This may mean sitting down after a long busy night and writing up a report for another couple of hours before they can get away to their beds.

For the daytime shifts, a traffic accident is a completely different kettle of fish. The one we attended in Osnabrück was probably typical.

A soldier recently returned from Bosnia was driving his large Army lorry across town. The car in front of him stopped at a set of lights, and he did not. He drove into the back of the car, caving in the boot and smashing all of its lights. Fortunately, the driver was unhurt. However, he was a German civilian and when he had recovered from the shock of what had happened, refused to move his car which was by now causing a nice little snarl-up. The RMP were called and spent a great deal of time trying to persuade the man to let them move his car aside. He still refused and insisted on waiting for the German civil police to arrive and record the details of the accident before he did so.

Just when the soldier thought it could not get any worse – he had run into the back of another vehicle, the driver was an irate German, the RMP had been called so now it would all be official – to make his day we happened to be driving past, so he had the full undivided attention of a BBC film crew to record every moment of his discomfort. His misery was further compounded when, having finally moved the vehicles and settled down with the German police to record his drivers' details, he discovered he did not have them with him.

Even the two RMP corporals who stood by began to feel sorry for him. They offered as much help as possible and reminded him that he had a choice about what would happen to him. He could either pay an on-the-spot fine to the German police or have the matter dealt with by his commanding officer. There was a long, detailed discussion about the pros and cons of each alternative, and the soldier seemed genuinely grateful for the help and support he was being given. The two RMP corporals were his only source of comfort and despite his predicament they finally managed to get a smile out of him.

By this time he had given up trying to hide his face from the camera and was completely absorbed in how he would explain this little mess to his unit

A soldier in need. An RMP corporal advises the unlucky driver who drove into the back of a German civilian's car.

once he finally returned to camp. We thought it might go something like 'Sarge, I've just bumped into this chap down town, never met him before, then I met the RMP and a BBC film crew . . .'

One of the most surprising things about the job of the RMP corporal is how often he is asked to provide a sympathetic ear or shoulder to cry on.

During our filming in Osnabrück we were called to attend a disturbance outside one of the bars. When we arrived we found a soldier in tears on the pavement, being comforted by his mate. The corporals questioned him and discovered that he had fallen out with his girlfriend during their evening and she had hit him. This had been rather public and he was not surprisingly rather upset about it. His best friend had persuaded him to leave, but once outside he had wanted to go back in and confront his girlfriend again.

There had been a brief tussle while the friend had tried to stop him and it had ended with the exchange of a few blows. The soldier had fallen down and banged his head on the side of a German taxi which was waiting outside. Fortunately his head was fine, but sadly the car was not. It was dented and the taxi driver was very annoyed about it. He insisted the RMP should be called so the matter could be reported in full and he would receive proper compensation.

The young soldier was by now quite distraught and the two corporals spent a great deal of time taking his details and trying to cheer him up. The young soldier seemed genuinely surprised that the hated 'Monkeys' were in fact human after all and was grateful for their help.

Eventually, the corporals got him into the patrol car and set off to get the soldier back to his barracks. When we arrived at the unit's gate he was duly handed over. We expected him to thank the two corporals before he left, but instead he turned his back on them and marched away.

When we questioned the corporals about the soldier's surprising change of heart, they explained that he would not want to have been seen being friendly with the RMP in front of his own unit. We asked whether that part of the job ever got them down and their reply was that it was all water off a duck's back.

However, we suspect that this is not quite the case. We have seen corporals who appear genuinely hurt by the abuse. One corporal told us that he did not mind the nicknames, but he did find it hard to accept the way the corps is expected to deal with all the awful jobs without any thanks or appreciation. He described having to attend a training accident where a couple of soldiers had been crushed by a tank. It had been his job to search through the bodies for identification. He had done so while all around had kept their distance. When he had finished he handed over what he had found to a senior officer and left. No one thanked him for doing a job nobody else wanted to do; they just assumed that the 'RMP would deal with it'.

Chapter 4

THE BRANCH

The Special Investigation Branch (SIB) does not wear uniform. Not khaki uniform anyway. It does wear another sort of uniform: blue pin-stripe suits, white shirts, ties and highly polished shoes. But the clothes allowance being as small as it is, a suit of any kind, provided it is formal, is tolerated.

On ceremonial occasions, like courts martial, SIB soldiers wear the SIB tie, dark blue with diagonal stripes (gold for officers, silver for other ranks), between which are spidery smudges, which, on closer inspection, are revealed as a nineteen-twigged branch. The wearing of the SIB tie is a coveted honour, not granted to anyone. At the time of writing, a high-ranking RMP officer, more an administrator than a detective, has let it be known that he would like to sport the tie. Legitimate wearers have voted to withhold the right, the officer in question having no track record as a sleuth – a cataclysmic insult equivalent to the University of Oxford refusing an honorary degree to Margaret Thatcher!

The device on the tie, and indeed on every notice-board outside every SIB office in the world, is a pun, 'the Branch' – the Army's equivalent of the plain-clothes CID – being represented by a branch of a tree. However, each twig of the branch represents a name, one of the original nineteen founder members of the SIB.

The origin of the modern SIB (something akin did exist from 1919–26) lies at the start of the Second World War. In 1939, the British sent an expeditionary force to France to prevent it being overrun by the Germans. However, the Germans need not have stirred themselves: the Allies were doing their job for them perfectly adequately. Gangs of British soldiers and civilians were pillaging and looting, there was a vigorous black market, and vehicles were arriving in forward positions completely stripped of their parts. The French police were powerless to help. In a sample week in Rennes, where 6,000

The symbol of the branch is conspicuous at SIB headquarters around the world, a constant reminder that today's large organization grew from a sapling of just nineteen.

British soldiers were stationed, there was a serious smash-and-grab, two armed robberies, six other substantial burglaries, fifteen cases of assault and criminal damage, and four stolen cars, one belonging to the Chief of Police.

It was an inglorious episode in British military history, and one which the authorities would not put up with for long. Accordingly, Detective Chief Inspector Hatherill vacated his desk at New Scotland Yard and visited the plundered towns of northern France. On the basis of what he saw there, Hatherill recommended the setting up of a task force from his own department in Scotland Yard. Volunteers were called for, and by mid-February 1940, nineteen policemen exchanged dark blue for khaki. After only two weeks in uniform, they left the Military Police Depot at Mytchett, arriving in Le Havre with a sketchy knowledge of the King's Regulations (the Army's Bible), and some rudimentary instructions in small arms. It was also thought necessary to instruct them in square-bashing. The policemen were: Harold Dibbens, Jack Ellie, George Hooper, Jimmy James, Frank Elliott, George West, Harry Green, William Heddon, Maurice Good, George Nicholls, Jimmy Rignall, George Ripley, Ernest Puslow, Albert Raisbeck, Frank Pollard, William Billyard, Ronald Crocker, Jimmy Coutts and George Baker.

There was a twentieth policeman, who is not commemorated by a twig on the branch – Det. Sup. Campion, gazetted Maj. C.E. Campion, the officer commanding the small force. Campion died in a Luftwaffe attack on Boulogne beach. He was ordering his sergeant to don a tin hat when he himself was hit in the head, having omitted to don his own. He was rushed to a field hospital, but it clearly was not his day – the hospital was hit as well, and there were no survivors. Campion was thus the first SIB martyr.

The leaderless men were deployed about the ever-shrinking British salient. According to a survivor of the original nineteen, George Ripley, the nascent SIB was not hugely successful, whatever the official overview. Reminiscing on those days in retirement in Paulton-le-Fyle, near Blackpool, Ripley vehemently denies that the English policemen-turned-soldiers made much headway at all against the thuggery and racketeering. Ripley had worked in Criminal Records, sifting through files to check on a suspect's criminal past, and liaising with the fingerprint department. Having lived in the comfortable and cosy world of Scotland Yard, he must have found the chaos and nervy atmosphere of a country on the verge of invasion something of a shock. Moreover, he could not speak French.

The SIB were in France for a mere four months, from 28 February to 18 June 1940. Ripley found the job impossible. He is tight-lipped about the degree of crime among British soldiers in the early years of the war ('I don't want to cause any trouble with the British Army'), preferring to concentrate on the misdeeds of the French dockers, who went about their nefarious practices, beyond the jurisdiction and linguistic capabilities of this fledgling gendarmerie. 'It was one thing getting out there,' he says, 'and quite another getting into the docks. I mean those docks were controlled by the French.'

By now the advancing German troops were in control of northern France, and criminal investigation was out of the question. The newly-formed SIB were absorbed into traffic control duties, and probably felt a good deal more at home. Well over 300,000 troops were evacuated from the Dunkirk beaches, and the surviving nineteen Special Investigators-turned-traffic-policemen

made their way back to England, reuniting at Mytchett.

It had been a baptism of fire in France, the job barely begun before it was finished. Back in England there was some debate as to whether it was worth persevering with the experiment of using civilian police as investigators within the military. It must have been a closely contested debate. Eventually, the authorities decided not to send the investigators back to their desks in Scotland Yard. They were deployed throughout Britain. It is from this decision that the SIB can confidently be said to have arrived.

As the SIB grew more experienced, confidence in it increased and its numbers steadily grew. Looking back fifty years it is tempting to conjure up a selfless crime-free Age of Innocence, single-mindedly dedicated to the overthrow of Hitler. The truth was more complex. The divorce rate in Britain was soaring. The crime rate went through the roof, particularly in the area of breaking and entering, where offences rose from 11,714 in 1939 to 21,260 in 1945. There was something particularly distasteful about the fact that the haves were leeching on the have-nots, that the robberies were on bombed houses or on the bodies of those killed in the blitz.

Just as George Ripley had found in Brest and St Nazaire, there was work to be done in the London docks. A vital component of the war effort were the Sherman tanks sent by the Americans, which arrived on boats that had run the gauntlet of U-boats across the Atlantic. When they left the United States they were sumptuously equipped. Inside were map-cases, binoculars, and even chocolate. But so comprehensively stripped were these tanks by English dockers, that only one ever got through intact.

Then there were shortages and rationing. There were those who were not prepared to exist on the stringent rations allowed by the Ministries, so market forces prevailed. Into the vacuum poured the spivs and the black market flourished. Home-based detectives during the war made quite a name for

The original nineteen members of the SIB, plus the officer commanding, Maj. Campion (centre) and staff officers.

themselves cracking rackets in bootleg War Department petrol, which was coloured pink to deter its illegal use, but which nevertheless was frequently stolen and put into civilian petrol tanks. Perhaps the SIB's finest moment was its interviewing of Rudolph Hess, Hitler's deputy, who landed in Britain in 1941 on a one-man peace mission.

The next foray abroad for the SIB was to Egypt in 1941 to support the desert campaigns. As in Britain and France, the wholesale plundering of supplies in Cairo, Alexandria and the Suez Canal was carried out by the native population with the connivance or active participation of British troops, either those on active service or those who had deserted from their units. These were called the 'Free British Corps' and the 'Dead-End Kids'. They were often from a criminal background in the UK and had been conscripted into the Army. They were responsible for an enormous number of weapons and ammunition thefts, and would ingratiate themselves with British soldiers with the sole purpose of stealing their weapons in an unguarded moment.

One right accorded to the SIB by the Egyptian Government in those days would never be allowed today – the right to kill thieves caught committing a theft of Army property. A large number were shot dead by the SIB at the great Ordnance Depot at Tel-el-Kebir; but for every thief caught hundreds went undetected. Lighters loaded with strategic supplies bound for the desert war against Rommel were deliberately capsized in the Suez Canal for retrieval by underwater booty snatchers under cover of dark. Foreshadowing Alan Bleasdale's classic 1980s television drama 'Boys from the Blackstuff', Royal Engineers took backhanders from local contractors for approving roads that were hardly more than tar sprayed on the desert. Badly needed lorries were 'targeted' by a clever system of forged documents and fake gate passes into the docks.

It was in the Middle East that the SIB came face to face for the first time with what has become one of the curses of the British Army: drugs. Opium and hashish from the Lebanon, bound for the teeming population of the Nile Delta, became an SIB target. It was the practice of drug dealers to bribe soldiers to take the drugs across the border in Army vehicles, because the soldiers were immune from search by the Egyptian anti-narcotic agency. In any study of the Redcaps it is hard to avoid the conclusion that there is no villainy, no ingenious scam beyond the imagination of the British soldier.

As the Allied war effort expanded, so the activities of the SIB increased. By 1944, they were in North Africa, Sicily and Italy, where they were again to tackle the familiar problems of banditry from deserters from the Allied armies. It was in Italy that a significant addition was made to the SIB portfolio – the investigation of war crimes – and this is still an SIB role. (Teams of SIB investigators compiled a comprehensive dossier on Iraqi atrocities in Kuwait in the early 1990s, and are awaiting the unlikely agree-

The British soldier was no saint. Gangs of deserters ran riot across war-torn Europe.

WANTED!

FOR ATTEMPTED MURDER AND ARMED ROBBERY

All Escaped from Custody in Naples on Night 3/4 July
Believed Travelling North

THIS IS PTE. COOPER

PHOTOGRAPH NOT AVAILABLE

THIS IS GNR. TOMLINSON

Pte COOPER	Gdsm BOOKER	Gnr TOMLINSON
Age 26	Age 27	Age 27
Height 5' 8"	Height 6' 2"	Height 5' 10"
Hair Dark Brown	Hair Dark Brown	Hair Blonde
Eyes Dark	Eyes Brown	Eyes Blue
Complexion Sallow	Complexion Dark	Complexion Fair
Build Slight	Build Good Bearing	Build Good Bearing
Cockney Accent	Moustache	Squint Left Eye
Scar on Left Cheek	Bushy Eyebrows	

Specialize in Armed Hold-ups of WD Vehicles, all types. Will not hesitate to shoot. If seen, or thought to have been seen, report facts **immediately** to nearest Provost or Unit Commander.

ment of Saddam Hussein for the extra-dition of those named. The SIB has also collected evidence of war crimes in Bosnia and Croatia since the early 1990s, and they will put all this data at the disposal of the newly constituted court in The Hague which in 1995 began prosecuting war criminals.)

The SIB arrived in Normandy on D+2 – two days after D-Day. In these early days of the liberation of Europe, detectives sometimes found themselves investigating self-inflicted wounds among soldiers in the front line. This is a ploy used by soldiers to get themselves medically discharged and so escape to a place of safety, at a time when it was by no means certain that the outcome of the invasion would be a happy one. The wound usually consisted of a disabling shot into the foot or the knee.

Nazi war criminals arrested after the Second World War. The picture in the centre of the bottom row shows an Italian partisan who was executed by the Nazis. These were the types of pictures used by the RMP for documentation purposes in the prosecution of war crimes.

Looked at from a cold SIB point of view rather than from the misty-eyed viewpoint of 'Their Finest Hour', the breach in Hitler's Atlantic Wall, which is what the Normandy landings achieved, was accompanied by the normal depressing rollcall of desertion, looting and theft. It gives no grounds for a patriotic tingle to learn that the SIB were brought in to investigate thefts from prisoners-of-war by British soldiers, even though perhaps one can feel some warped admiration for the entrepreneurial spirit of the soldier who sold his Bren gun carrier to a French farmer for £100. The farmer used it as a plough.

If there is one motif that runs like a virus through the war years, it is the black market. At a time of unimaginable austerity, the NAAFI and Army Ordnance Corps depots were oases of plenty, goods reaching astronomical prices on the black market in cash or kind. To poorly paid servicemen the temptations were too great. Once more the SIB found itself in conflict with organized gangs of thieves, many of whom were deserters who would not hesitate to murder if necessary.

These criminals were not exclusively British. During the war, Albert Pierrepoint, the official hangman, was assigned to hang a batch of rogue American soldiers. 'We hanged twenty-two Yanks in one morning,' he said. 'They'd got people all over the place who had been sentenced to death in this country and in Europe. They brought them all to Shepton Mallet in Somerset, where they had a big military prison. We did the lot in one morning. It was a production line. Shout the name out. Bring the man in. Read the crime and sentence. Drop. Down the pit. Check from the doctor. Get them off the rope. Re-set the trap and adjust the rope. Next one. We had no trouble. We had two bloody great American military policemen on the job just in case, but there wasn't anything serious. They had to carry one or two in because they were almost fainting and couldn't walk . . . They paid us for each man. Cash on the nail. In dollars! I've never had such a pocketful of money, and I couldn't spend it.'

In the NAAFI stores in Germany today there is a lingering reminder of those far-off days of racketeering and the black market. Soldiers and their wives are still to be seen at the checkout passing ration books across to checkout girls who cancel coupons for butter, tea, coffee and whisky – the priceless barter items of the 1940s – which in the newly unified Germany are still anomalously rationed. One almost expects a man with a gaudy tie and a pencil moustache to sidle up and murmur out of the side of his mouth, 'Psst, want any nylons?'

Postwar, the SIB were to be found wherever there were British soldiers: in West Germany, Berlin, Palestine, Malaya, Korea, East Africa, Egypt, Cyprus and Aden. Very roughly, there is one SIB investigator to every thousand soldiers. Today, SIB operatives are the brains of the RMP. They have all done their time as Redcaps, as 'coppers on the beat'. They know all about patrolling, traffic duties, minor domestic tiffs and nicking drunks. But Redcaps with ambition for a fuller, more varied life apply to join the Branch. Transfer is not automatic. Would-be investigators serve six months' probation in a SIB unit, and only when the candidate has the recommendation of the officer commanding will he or she go on to a bewildering series of courses, both at the RMP Depot in Chichester and with civilian forces outside: scenes of crime, photography, fingerprints, drugs, surveillance techniques, forensic, and the law, civil and military. When all these hurdles are surmounted the military policeman or woman will transfer permanently to the Branch as a sergeant.

It is dangerous to jump to hasty conclusions about other people's jobs, but one can confidently say that the civil police must look at their military counterparts with some envy. Though not in terms of hardware – we were shocked at how poorly equipped the RMP were. Their cars were ancient and unreliable; their radios in this modern age laughably primitive. In Germany, Redcaps on patrol kept small change in their pockets because the car phones could not be relied on to make contact with the police station three miles away and the only way to communicate was by public phone. More than once Redcaps used our cameraman's mobile phone to contact base.

Where the Redcaps and the SIB have an incalculable advantage over the civil police is that each soldier has an identity card, and each soldier's details and record and address are on file at the RMP Computer Centre in Lillie Road, Fulham (since the time of writing, the Centre has moved to the RMP Depot at Chichester, in May 1995). The Computer Centre is open twenty-four hours a day all year around to authorized enquirers - usually the provost companies and SIB units.

The Army is not a huge organization anymore. In 1995, it consisted of only 123,028 souls (115,976 men and 7,052 women). By and large they live in military communities, which are like little ghettos scattered throughout the length and breadth of the country. In the barracks, in the married quarters complexes, everybody knows everybody else, and their business. Living among them are military policemen, who not only know the psychology of the soldier, the sort of person he is and the sort of thing he gets up to, but have access to the data in the RMP computer. The first thing an SIB investigator will do if he has the name of a suspect is to dial up the number of the Crime Computer Records, and tap in the name of the suspect. Let us assume it is Richardson. Up on the screen will come all the Richardsons in the British Army, name, initial, date of birth, rank, number and regiment. A further code targeting a particular Richardson will reveal whether the suspect has had any brushes with authority, trivial or serious, and whether he or she has any special characteristics, tattoos being a favourite.

Recently, the SIB in Aldershot contacted the Computer Centre to help them on a rape enquiry. A woman had been sexually assaulted by the side of the Basingstoke Canal, which runs through the Aldershot Garrison. The computer came up with thirteen possible suspects, later cut down to a short-list of four, and this resulted in the arrest by the police of an ex-serviceman. The soldier had been serving in Northern Ireland when he was accidentally shot through the thigh. The bullet exited through his other thigh, but in its passage had severed his penis. In subsequent medical treatment doctors had tried to rebuild the penis, but he was unable to achieve an erection. All this was noted by the SIB in Northern Ireland and held on the data base in London. It is just one example of the exceptional detail kept on each British soldier, and it prompts the layman to the conclusion that the Army police are well ahead of the civilian police in the way they can keep tabs on and control the Army. Indeed, with the advantages it has at its disposal one feels the SIB should be able to crack every crime committed by soldiers, whether on other soldiers or on civilians.

Maj. Frank Lindop, MBE, on another lengthy phonecall.

About a quarter of the filming for the BBC series took place at the SIB section in Imphal Barracks, York. This section's patch is Eastern Command, which stretches far from the north of England, taking in the huge camp complex of Catterick in North Yorkshire, down the eastern side to the old Roman garrison town of Colchester.

The official title of this section is 33 Section SIB RMP UKLF (the Army loves to talk in acronyms and capital letters wherever possible). It had been on no recce itinerary that the Army had planned for us, but we heard by chance that the officer commanding, Maj. Frank Lindop, was interested in amateur dramatics. This immediately marked him out as an unusual military policeman, as on the whole we found them friendly but clannish, with few outside interests beyond the job, their families and quiet introvert hobbies. Frank Lindop is tall and upright. He was born in Hastings, the third son of a farmer from the Crewe area. He went straight from school into the Metropolitan Police, and very soon into the RMP. Like all the most effective SIB officers, he has risen from the ranks. He has a penetrating *basso profundo* voice, and a deep resonant laugh. He is kindly, but it would not be enjoyable to be interviewed by him. His eyes could bore straight into a guilty conscience. His sentences are punctuated by repeated formulae. A favourite expression is 'there's no doubt about that at all'. We once heard him say, when surprised, 'Well, I'll eat my red hat with gravy!'

We never discovered whether Frank Lindop actually trod the boards, but we quickly ascertained that he was a man whose mind had not atrophied with the passing years, and whose interests were wide and ever-expanding. He was a keen glider pilot when we first met, but abandoned that when an acquaintance died in a crash caused by a rogue thermal. Frank Lindop cultivates his garden in a sunlit gallery outside his office – tomatoes in pots and exotic shrubs which he sprays lovingly as he thinks of crime and punishment. For those seeking an audience, he leaves only one book to read as he embarks on lengthy phonecalls – the collected poems of Rudyard Kipling. He will, if encouraged, launch into a paeon of praise for Kipling, and will quote from the *Barrack Room Ballads*. Kipling, he says, understood soldiers, and has no equal among writers on military themes. This year, Maj. Lindop and his wife went to India, not to flop on some beach in Goa, but to explore the cultural diversity and contradictions of the sub-continent.

Frank Lindop is something of a maverick figure among his peers. They are not quite sure what to make of him, and mention of his name will provoke sidelong glances, a raised eyebrow. Frank seems happiest among young detectives as a guru, a teacher, and a father figure. He takes positive pleasure in their success, and he delights in helping someone in trouble. A young detective who had drunk too much on a cross-channel ferry and had committed certain indiscretions, was under Frank's benign supervision while the filming was taking place. That detective benefited from the experience, has surmounted a serious setback, and is now well launched on what everyone assumes will be a successful career.

As mentioned in the Foreword, there is a widespread fear of the media in the Army, which has never really recovered from William Howard Russell's shocking eye-witness despatches to *The Times* during the Crimean War, but Frank Lindop was prepared to give us the benefit of the doubt. And he carried the rest of his SIB section with him, although some of them had reservations and were waiting for their worst suspicions to be confirmed. We were 'auditioned' at the Gimcrack – a large roadhouse on the Fulford Road – at one of those seemingly innocent social occasions when one is being appraised by all present for accent, demeanour, attitude, was-he-a-luvvy?, could-he-take-his-beer? We agreed to begin filming a fortnight later. There was no plan. We would pitch up at the SIB headquarters. It was a fire-brigade operation.

When we arrived (producer, cameraman and sound-recordist), we were allocated a waiting-cum-reception room in which to store our gear. There were seats around the room, a large map on the wall, a fridge (usually empty), a sink, a kettle, some coffee and tea bags. We contributed coffee and biscuits. House rules were that we could walk into any office whose door was open, but a closed door, like a 'sported oak' in an Oxford College, meant 'no entry'.

If there is one expression that grates on the film-maker, it is 'fly on the wall'. It is quite impossible for a crew to be 'invisible'. However, if it hangs around long enough, it can become 'part of the furniture', and it was to achieve this that our vigil in York began.

We were immediately faced with a brain-numbingly labyrinthine fraud in which a clever warrant officer had embezzled a huge but unknown sum of money. Such was the complexity of the fraud – known in the business as 'teaming and lading' – that it was beyond the generalists at SIB York, and Sgt

Maj. (WO1) Mick Richardson had been whistled up from the Special Operations unit in Old Sarum. Spec. Ops Unit is a group of specialist teams that was originally set up in 1992 in a lovely old manor house near Salisbury. Richardson's small outfit was the Army equivalent of the Serious Fraud Office, and he himself had spent all his Army career in the Royal Army Pay Corps, before it merged into the Adjutant General's Corps in 1992. Mick Richardson can read a set of accounts like a book. He has run such accounts himself, audited them, and instructed Pay Corps personnel on how to handle them. There was an extra moral dimension to Richardson's investigation. The fraudulent pay clerk was also Pay Corps trained. 'We were supposed to be professionals,' said Richardson, bitterly. 'I feel he's let the side down. You know, there's a basic *esprit de corps*.' Meanwhile, the subject of the investigation was hardly helping the police with their enquiries. Although Mick Richardson could prove that fraud had taken place, there was no trace of where the money had gone, and the suspect was not saying. It was certainly not in any of his known bank accounts; he had no mistress; he did not gamble. Frank Lindop and Mick Richardson spent hours, days together, agonizing over the sequestered account books. The answer had to lie somewhere in all that paper . . .

By a curious coincidence the very next job also involved fraud. Already it was becoming all too apparent that the opportunities to line pockets at the taxpayers' expense are as rife today as they were when the SIB was set up over fifty years ago. There are many different funds and accounts for different purposes with different layers of supervision, any one of which, if bent, can result in fraud. Just before our arrival, the SIB in York had uncovered a profitable fiddle. At the time of the Gulf War, some soldiers launched an appeal for 'Treats for our Troops' in a local newspaper. Gifts in cash and kind were solicited, and they poured in, including 7,000 Sony Walkmans from a local factory. No treats ever arrived for the troops. The goods were sold in a large anonymous car-boot sale in the wolds of Lincolnshire.

But today we were going to the Army School of Mechanical Transport at Leconfield, from where disquieting reports had reached the ears of the SIB in York. It appeared that things were not quite as they should have been with regard to the NAAFI rebate fund run by a retired major. Every month the NAAFI sends back to each unit a percentage – usually about five per cent – of the profits it has made on its business activities in the unit. The monthly NAAFI cheque should be banked and used for welfare purposes, for anything from new ping-pong balls to building projects. At Leconfield, the sums involved were sizeable, varying between £3,000 and £6,000 a month.

Armed with data supplied by the NAAFI going back to July 1992 SSgt Howard Wright and SSgt Mark Bent drive into the camp, introduce themselves to the CO, and without ado march straight into the office of the startled fund-holder, who is poring over large ledgers. SSgt Bent begins: 'Sir, we have got some information that there may be some irregularities within the accounting for NAAFI rebates. We are not pointing fingers, but we have to act on this information. We propose to check to see that you have brought the cheques to account . . .' adding unnecessarily 'if you don't mind.' The retired major, who is in a uniform that bears the insignia of a respected cavalry regiment now merged into extinction, is urbanity itself. 'Help yourself, dear boy,' he murmurs, and leaves the two detectives to check the information supplied by the NAAFI against entries in the account book.

The checking is thorough but not exhaustive. Both soldiers are aware that if there are irregularities, there will be no court martial. As the major has retired from the armed services, and he is therefore technically a civilian, this will be a case for the civilian police.

However, there is to be no case at all. Whoever whispered to York that something was wrong in Leconfield, had got it wrong himself. The major's book-keeping was punctilious. The two policemen informed him that everything was in order, and the major could not resist a Parthian shot. 'Was it "Bent", you said you were called?' he said to the sergeant. 'Yes,' SSgt Bent replied. 'Unfortunate name for a policeman, don't you think?'

The two detectives tried to put a good face on it, but after so much legwork, they would not have been human if they had not felt a tiny pang of disappointment. An arrest is after all a scalp. However, sounding slightly unconvincing, the SIB explains that proving someone above suspicion is just as important as nicking him, and that the day's work is not wasted. It has been 'pro-active', 'crime-preventative'. As SSgt Wright explains, 'The word will have got out that the SIB have been in. The Officers' Mess this lunch-time will be buzzing. "The SIB has been looking at the books." Anybody running a similar account will think twice before doing anything illegal, so it should prevent crime.'

This was hardly the crime of the century. In fact it was not a crime at all. It didn't require great Holmesian leaps of imagination and deduction, merely the comparing of entries of money paid out against entries of money received. But that moment when the major was caught off his guard was high drama, with all the undertones of class and rank, the icy cordiality, the unspoken threat, and the possibility of disgrace.

It would be unfair to say that Maj. Lindop stood aloof from the day-to-day caseload. It was rather that he was happy to delegate the minutiae. There were plenty of policy matters to occupy his time, and he spent many hours in the company of Lt. Col. Dick Austin of the Army Legal Service (the ALS – the Army equivalent of the Crown Prosecution Service) or Bill McGinty (major, retired) the GI officer in charge of discipline, and a man well-versed in military law and court martial procedure. Lindop would talk on the phone to them for hours, or, if there was something deeply preoccupying, he would stroll across the attractive lawns of Imphal Barracks to Headquarters Building (McGinty) or the rather incongruous suburban semi which the ALS shares with the medics.

Today Lindop had left Sgt Dawn Phillips investigating a bullying incident (last year there were a hundred reported cases in the Army worldwide), Sgt Mark Bent looking into the theft of fifty-six tool-boxes worth £30,000, Sgt Maj. Karen Miller setting up a surveillance operation on a soldier suspected of selling pornography from married quarters in Colchester, and Sgt Sue Sheridan on the track of two soldiers in the Green Howards in Catterick selling fake tax discs and MOT certificates for £30 each. Lindop is preoccupied with a conundrum. According to his information, the CO of a regiment in Germany may have perverted the course of justice. Yet this is by definition impossible, as the CO is himself the justice.

It appears that a private in the Prince of Wales Own Regiment, involved in a love tangle with a corporal's wife, was set upon and attacked by the aggrieved husband and an accomplice. The private complained to the authorities, saying at the same time that he wanted out of the Army. It was alleged that the Prince of Wales Own also wanted this private 'out of the family', and the whole matter swept under the carpet. It was put to the private that if he pressed charges of grievous bodily harm, it would have to go to court martial, a lengthy process with an uncertain outcome. Whereas, if he would admit to 'fighting', it would be an internal matter, he would be locked up in the regimental guard room for a few weeks, and the CO would look sympathetically on his application for a discharge. It is a strong-minded soldier indeed who goes against the system. There are plenty of cases of men who have inadvisedly gone along with regimental 'advice', only to find they have subsequently disqualified themselves from substantial compensation. Predictably, the private did as he was advised.

But Frank Lindop was not happy with plea-bargaining. 'And,' he said, 'the PM (the Provost-Marshal) won't be happy about this either.' There were various courses of action open. The easiest was to do nothing. The Green Machine would be aghast at a major in the SIB rocking the boat. While the CO, a lieutenant colonel, was never going to be punished as such, there were subtler ways of administering a rap over the knuckles, and a second course open would be to ensure that the officer is summoned to 'an interview without coffee' with the brigadier. Meanwhile, Sgt Watkins is sent on a delicate diplomatic mission to the Prince of Wales Own Depot in Osnabrück, to find out whether all correct procedures have been complied with, and to ascertain what legal advice the CO had received, and indeed whether the plea-bargain was put to the private by his CO, or, in his absence, by the adjutant, his second-in-command.

Behind Lindop's pursuit of the matter was not some mischievous desire 'to put a bee in the bonnet of the system', but a realization of the growing importance of European legislation, and that if the Army cannot or will not put its house in order, then some European court will. This is already becoming a real issue with regard to homosexuals. All the service chiefs fear that European court rulings will compel them one day to drop the ban on gays in the armed forces.

Days pass. A steady trickle of cases passes across the RSM's desk . . . cannabis discovered in the possession of a soldier on guard duty at Catterick . . . a soldier rings his mother to say he's killed someone with an icepick, but there is no body, and the soldier was probably on a bad LSD trip . . . then there is a *real* murder – one of the thirty-eight that took place in 1994. Frank Lindop is on the road to Colchester.

Few murders are fascinating. Most are alcohol- or sex-related. Domestic *crimes passionelles* or killings resulting from booze-induced anger. This murder fell roundly into the second category: a brawl after closing-time outside a soldiers' pub in Colchester between some local yobs well-known to the police and a group of servicemen. A soldier lies dead. The assailants are easily identified, and are picked up quickly by the Essex police, charged and locked up. The case involves civilians and is therefore in the hands of the civil police. Frank Lindop's role is more liaison than detection. As for filming the enquiry and the crucial interface between the civilian and military authorities, the Essex police are even worse than the Green Machine. They refuse all cooperation.

The opportunity for the SIB to be sole investigator of a murder is comparatively rare. In the UK the matter would always be delegated to the civilian police; overseas it is more complex. Basically, if servicemen or dependants murder other servicemen or dependants it is a case for the SIB; but if servicemen or dependants murder civilians or are murdered by civilians, the case is taken up by the national police force of the country in which the murder took place. When the body of a Danish tour operator was found in Cyprus in 1994 and three Royal Green Jackets soldiers were arrested, the subsequent enquiries were handled by the Cypriot police under Cypriot law.

When we next see Frank Lindop he is almost purring at an elegant piece of detective work by the ex-Pay Corps Warrant Officer, Mick Richardson, in pursuit of the bent pay clerk who had been 'teaming and lading'. A weakness in the SIB case has always been that there has never been any trace of the money in the suspect's bank account, but Richardson has been looking at some jottings on a piece of paper taken from the pay clerk's desk when he was arrested. They looked bank-numberish, although they were not an actual bank number. Once more the RMP computer is pressed into service. The suspect's service career is reconstructed, and a note taken of where he banked his service pay. Immediately the spotlight falls on Germany. There is only one digit different between the jotting on the desk and the sorting code and account number of the Dresdner Bank in Detmold, where the suspect had once banked. Soldiers are instructed to close all bank accounts before leaving Germany, but clearly the suspect had not done so. It is simple, though expensive, to transfer money to Germany, and that is clearly what he had done.

But it will not be easy to have a look at this account. Data protection in Germany is strict. However, all experienced detectives have a network of acquaintances in useful places built up over the years, and they are all owed favours. Frank Lindop has served in Germany; he has a friend who is a bank manager; he also has contacts in the Kripo (the German CID). Alternatively, he could make an official application, through the convenor of the court that could try the suspect, to make an order requiring the bank to release details of the account. Failing all else he could go to the suspect himself and try to sweet-talk him into authorizing Mick Richardson to look at the account.

All else did fail. Not surprisingly, the suspect withheld his permission for any detective to examine the Detmold bank account. For the time being, deadlock.

Much of the time, Frank Lindop ponders the application of PACE, the Police and Criminal Evidence Act, which governs the conduct of the police in its dealings with suspects and which came into force after the wrongful conviction of the Birmingham Six. PACE applies as much to the RMP as civilian police forces. Heaven knows what happened in SIB interview rooms before the act became law. Given the authoritarian nature of the military and its deference to higher rank, many a confession – whether true or false – must have been given under the sort of pressure the act seeks to eliminate. With PACE in place, the bad old ways are supposed to have gone. All Frank Lindop's investigators must be modern detectives, not old-fashioned. 'We must "Think Defence",' he says. 'We are not in the business of pursuing a confession. We are in the business of seeking an explanation.'

Arrested soldiers are treated considerately in Frank Lindop's police station. The articles of PACE are performed to the letter, as indeed they are in all SIB premises. Two tapes in the tape recorder, the caution, the rights of the arrested person to consult a legal advisor and to have a legal advisor present during the interview explained, the suspect's attention drawn to a red folder in front of him called 'The Service Police Codes of Practice', the handing over of MoD Form 811A entitled 'Notice to Suspect', which explains the suspect's rights. Only then does the interview begin, and this must not be overbearing, pressurizing, sarcastic or oppressive. The suspect may not be called back for a second interview about the same charge, unless some new evidence comes to light. Throughout the RMP there was scandalized indignation at the scene in Channel 4's 'Cutting Edge' programme, 'Navy Blues', where the naval equivalent of the SIB turns off the tape, and proceeds to bully the suspect. It was particularly galling to the RMP as the naval investigators had been trained at the RMP Depot at Chichester, and appeared not to have appreciated even the first principle taught there, which is that the purpose of the investigation is not to exact a confession, but to elicit facts and explanations, and leave it to the court martial to decide on guilt and innocence.

In the preliminary investigation of the Birmingham Six, the forensic team took swabs from the suspects, some of which were submitted as evidence, some not. The defence later found that it would have based its defence on the swabs that were not disclosed. The lessons of the Birmingham Six have been well learned; the rules for disclosure to the defence are now draconian. 'I must be prepared to disclose everything,' said Frank Lindop, adding, perhaps fancifully, 'even my own thoughts'. Certainly, each member of the filming crew had to declare his presence aloud to the tape recorder at the start of whatever interview he was permitted to attend. We were also advised to write down all conversations with suspects just in case we were called to give evidence.

At a press conference in the summer of 1994, the Commissioner of the Metropolitan Police, Sir Paul Condon, launched 'Operation Safety Catch'. Sadly, he said, there were on average one or two shots a day fired from illegal firearms on the streets of London. This was a dangerous situation which had to be halted. The public was given a telephone number to ring. No questions would be asked. Then Commander Bill Griffiths of the Met added that the source of firearms were burglaries from authorized owners, unscrupulous arms dealers and military sources.

At about this time, two soldiers on R and R from Bosnia are overheard talking in a pub in Scunthorpe. They have AK47 assault rifles for sale. The conversation is reported to Humberside Police, who contact the SIB in York. Frank Lindop takes charge of the case. Immediately, the RMP computer is put to work. Could the computer trawl through all serving soldiers who have served in Bosnia with a Scunthorpe or Lincolnshire connection, however tenuous? Next day the printout arrives. It is about nineteen inches high and weighs a ton. Sgt Dawn Phillips – the most junior investigator – is given the task of checking tens of thousands of names.

If the field could be narrowed even more, clearly her load would be lightened. Frank Lindop has a hunch. Shipping Kalashnikovs out of Bosnia is much easier if they are driven out in lorries or secreted in tanks. But an arms smuggler would avoid x-ray machines, for example at airports. That would point to a unit whose home base is Germany. Names from garrisons in Belize, Hong Kong and Cyprus can therefore be eliminated, as can all women, and following a description of the two men in the Scunthorpe pub, all men over thirty-five. This does not significantly reduce the numbers. Most soldiers are male, under thirty-five, and serving in the UK and Germany. Dawn Phillips starts work on a printout only marginally less daunting than the first. But Frank Lindop's thinking is sound. We watched the Redcaps at work in the British Military Base in Vitez in Bosnia, searching tea-chests of the 2nd Royal Anglian Regiment ('The Poachers') that were full of non-essential gear returning to the regimental base at Celle in Germany after their six months deployment. Cpl Peter Lavery found a Bosnian bayonet in a tea-chest that turned out to be a souvenir that a Royal Anglian captain was smuggling out. He was later fined £100 by his CO, but what struck the lay observer was the number of tea-chests – hundreds – and the likelihood that only a token few could be searched. Whatever was in the rest would be waved through at border crossings.

Dawn is on her own. The remainder of the section are at York Races circulating among the punters or high up in the grandstand scanning the crowds with binoculars for a corporal and six accomplices who have decided to spend a day at the races with a wad of counterfeit banknotes they propose to launder through the bookies.

Then there is a breakthrough. From the CID comes the initial of the man's name: H. Dawn Phillips' marker-pen hovers over a name and stops. Private H (name withheld) of 2 Royal Anglian, based in Germany, currently on UN duties in Bosnia, with an address in the Scunthorpe area. It is a textbook solution, classically and cleanly executed. Next day, the Humberside CID, with the SIB RSM Kevin Morson in attendance, arrests Private H. By his bed is a 9 mm Browning revolver and a dangerous looking machete. Private H is brought back to Imphal Barracks and locked up in the guardroom while enquiries continue. Private H's belongings are searched by the Redcaps in Bosnia and Germany. Twenty-two rounds of AK47 ammunition are discovered, which is good news – and bad news. Good news because a dangerous weapon and some bullets have been taken off the streets; bad news because it suggests that there *were* AK47s, which may by now have been sold on.

To the fury of those who had spent so many hours tracking him to earth and to the astonishment of more senior officers in the RMP, no action has been taken against Private H. No one knows why, and until there is a convincing reply, the SIB will believe it is simply laziness on the part of the Army Legal Service in Germany, that in the midst of 'Operation Safety Catch', when the Metropolitan Police was worried about firearms getting into the wrong hands from military sources, a soldier, caught apparently red-handed, walked away scot-free.

The SIB – particularly the older investigators, who have done the rounds of military postings – are good company, with a mine of tragic, humorous, often stomach-churning, anecdotes.

One of the pleasures of filming in Hohne, Germany, with 70 Section SIB ('The Fighting Seventieth' as its OC calls it) is the time when there is no filming.

It is something of a privilege to sit in the '31 Club', a snug little bar festooned with plaques from other units and police forces, knocking back Beck's beer at knock-down prices, listening to the professionals relaxing at the end of their day (one SIB junior is detailed to remain sober during the symposium; he has to drive). It is a very masculine atmosphere.

The sergeant major, Barry Philbin, produces a copy of the soft-porn magazine Fiesta, Volume 28 issue 5. Among the naked ladies is a group photograph of naked soldiers of C Squadron, The Light Dragoons, dressed only in blue UN berets, flak jackets and boots, sent from Bosnia with a letter daring the magazine to print the picture, which of course it did. The SIB have been asked to look into the matter. It is reprehensible behaviour; the regiment's name has been dragged in the mud; charges might follow. The magazine was soon unobtainable at the Army bases. All copies were snapped up by the army wives, or so the story went.

The subject changes to post-mortems. A female SIB sergeant has come into the bar. She looks pale but eager to talk. Overseas, the SIB are the agents for the coroner in the case of Army deaths, and she had had to cope with the emotionally draining aftermath of a traffic accident.

One of the officers capped all the stories and reduced the room to silence with a horrific post-mortem he had attended. An SAS parachutist had been killed on exercise in Borneo. Although his body, entangled in his parachute harness, was in thick jungle, it was recovered and brought back to the nearest medical station. But by this time some days had elapsed, and the corpse was

Vitez, Bosnia. Cpl Peter Lavery discovers a Bosnian bayonet illegally secreted in an Anglian Regt tea-chest bound for Germany. Such 'souvenirs' are strictly forbidden.

Dangerous weapons: 9 mm Browning revolver and machete illegally smuggled into the UK by a Royal Anglian Regt private.

decomposing. Nevertheless, a post-mortem had to take place, and just as operations were about to begin, there was a power cut. All electrical sawing operations had to be performed by hand. The narrator of the story was detailed to assist the Army surgeon by holding the putrescent body as the top of the head was sawn off so that the brain could be examined. The details that followed are unmentionable.

It is not surprising that many SIB men have a cynical, almost world-weary approach to life. They have seen it all, done it all. They have observed their fellow men and women at their worst. Drunk, drugged, crazed, consumed with desire or jealousy. Whereas probably ninety per cent of the Army is composed of decent law-abiding folk, the SIB only see the ten per cent who are not. They have seen the innocent punished, the guilty rewarded. They have seen the murders, the suicides, and the tragic accidents on the roads and the ranges. They have confronted rapists and listened patiently to their distraught victims, spent long hours on stake-outs, and wrestled with the intricacies of fraud. As the Army contracts, one would expect the crime figures to lessen proportionately. That seems not to be happening, perhaps bearing out the Frank Lindop dictum: 'If we doubled our numbers in the SIB, we would find double the crimes.' Or, put another way, 'If we halved the numbers in the Army, the SIB would *still* find the same number of crimes.'

CHAPTER 5

POINTING PERCY AT THE PORCELAIN

They are easy to spot, the squaddies in town for a good night out. The short haircuts are a give-away, and there is something very uniform about their civilian clothes. North of England accents ricochet around the dim alleyways, and a burst of British laughter explodes on a cruel wisecrack as the group – the pack-instinct is strong among British soldiers – passes a particularly ugly prostitute behind plate-glass.

The Bulldog 'coffee shop', Amsterdam. More than coffee is for sale.

The scene is Amsterdam's red-light zone, Oudezijds Voorburgwal, and the streets and lanes that radiate off it. This zone of tolerance, where Europe's pleasure-seekers can let their hair down, is only a few hours' drive from Britain's garrison in what was West Germany. There are pornographic books to suit every taste, pornographic cinemas, live sex shows, and hundreds of prostitutes along the canals on display in glass cases, like butterflies. And there are drugs.

Since 1976, the sale and use of small quantities of soft drugs has been tolerated in Holland. To be in possession is considered a misdemeanour and rarely prosecuted in Amsterdam, although some authorities in more conservative areas can be sterner.

Since the 1976 law was introduced, hundreds of 'coffee shops' have opened in Amsterdam. Numbers vary; some say 450, but others will quote 1,000. Coffee shop is of course a euphemism. While these establishments do indeed serve coffee, it is for the hashish and marijuana that many enter the premises. It is easy to distinguish them from drug-free cafés. They are often adorned with brightly-coloured murals in which the Jamaican musician Bob Marley features prominently. They may display the cannabis leaf motif in the decor and they may well be in a street where there are shops selling the impedimenta of

Inside the Bulldog. A sale of marijuana is made, watched by a concealed camera. A misdemeanor under Dutch law, rarely prosecuted.

drug-taking: fancy cigarette papers for rolling, miniature hookahs, scales for weighing small amounts of drugs, and T-shirts, postcards and posters of weird graphic effects. The visual displays are supplemented by a battery of loudspeakers, from which pours a continual and mesmeric stream of heavy metal tracks that make conversation impossible.

The coffee shops may not advertise. They are closed to those under eighteen, and for their own self-preservation, they frown on traffic in hard drugs. They are allowed to have on the premises, and for sale, a small quantity of soft drugs. 'A small quantity' is defined as thirty grams. The legal restraint is meaningless. Asked what happens if twenty customers want two grams each, one coffee house proprietor, who described himself as a former Marseilles gangster, said, 'We just go to our store and get some more to replenish supplies.'

To purchase hashish or marijuana, a customer must go to the counter and ask for the menu. This may well be lying face down right in front of him in order to honour the no-advertising ban. The menu will be split into hashish, and the different varieties and provenances will be listed – Moroccan, Afghan, Nepalese, Turkish, Kashmiri, Lebanese and the home-produced Nederhash. Dutch marijuana is also very popular and there are imported varieties from Africa, Colombia and Thailand. The atmosphere in the coffee shops is friendly and unthreatening. They are crowded with spaced-out, happy young people, many of them British. For the green-fingered grass-smoker there is a shop specializing in the sale and cultivation of marijuana. It promotes a kind of vegetable show, with tips to gardeners on how to grow perfect marijuana plants.

Outside the coffee shops a more sinister work-force is at hand with a harder alternative. Acid, amphetamines, cocaine, crack, Ecstasy and heroin, all of dubious quality, are available and promoted with as much vigour as the spielers who leerily urge the groups of young men through doors advertizing 'Live Sex'.

Amsterdam's free and easy attitude to drugs and sex has had a dramatic effect on its appearance as citizens of sterner regimes have choked the narrow alleys and canal pavements to nibble or munch or gorge themselves on the forbidden fruit. Some of these are soldiers, enjoying a weekend away from their soldierly duties in the great barrack-concentrations of the British Army in northern Germany – Hohne in the north, Osnabrück in the centre, and Rheindahlen in the south.

With his own car and money to burn, the private soldier of today would not be recognized by the men who fought in the Second World War. It is quite likely that today's squaddie will come from a background where drug-taking is the norm. If he does not, there will be peer-pressure on him to adopt a sympathetic attitude, or he will be labelled a 'wimp'. A young man rising eighteen wants nothing more than to conform to his age-group. He will also almost certainly be bored. Gone are the days when the soldier in Germany can look in his shaving mirror at 06:30 hrs and see himself as one link in the thin khaki chain protecting Western Germany from being overrun by the Red Army. As he stares into his own reflection today, he must ask, 'What am I doing here?' What am I protecting? What am I protecting it from?' As if to confirm his worst suspicions, the Treasury gives the Government's tacit answer. There is enough money available to permit a soldier to go on a week's exercise *once* every *two years*. Exercises cost money, and it is cheaper not to use the tanks, cheaper to leave the shells unfired, cheaper not to pay the German authorities their fees for use of the firing ranges . . . The cutbacks have hit training hard. But the soldiers are still there, and they still have to do something.

If the squaddie turns on the radio to listen to BFBS (the British Forces Broadcasting Service), to see if there is anything worthwhile to do in his ample time off, this is what a typical week's leisure activities might sound like: 'Hohne's aerobic queen restarts her fitness classes; the REME Marathon (open to all cap badges) takes place; bingo at the Round House with a jackpot standing at 900 marks; a car-boot sale, and a 36-hole golf competition; a coffee morning for the wives of the Queen's Royal Hussars; Fallingbostel Martial Arts Club re-opens; and the education centre there will be running courses in dress-making, German cookery, German language, typing and mathematics.

This list of events is entirely resistable to the average eighteen-year-old. Many units seem to close down for the weekend at 12.30 on Fridays, except for those on guard duty. An observer outside the camp gates on Friday lunchtime will witness something approaching a Gadarene rush towards the autobahns.

The situation in Bosnia is quite different. In Vitez and Gornji Vakuf, where most of the British forces are, soldiers are in effect confined to barracks, and due to the alcohol limitation of two cans of beer per man per day there is very little of the crimes and misdemeanours that bedevil military communities in non-operational zones. But any suggestion that soldiers have too much money and too much spare time is rejected, not just by soldiers themselves, but also the authorities. The Devil might find work for idle hands, but it is the soldiers' inalienable right to dice with him, if they so desire.

Whether a rave can be defined as 'the Devil's work' is debatable. But certainly to anyone over the age of thirty-five it is a hellish enough experience. Visually, the rave's external aspect is temptingly infernal. Sometimes lasers light up the night sky, beacons to travellers on to which they can home, or, like lighthouses, a warning to keep away.

Inside, it is clear, to a jaundiced ear and eye, that no one is there for the subtlety of the music, which is loud, repetitive and monotonous, or for conversation, which would have to take place at maximum bellow. It is hot, relentless, other-worldish. To a lay observer, the sexes do not seem sexually interested in each other, but instead are caught up in some communal hypnotic experience that owes something to the presence of the drug Ecstasy. It is hot, and the noise and the heat and the drugs have sent some young hearts into overdrive and death. The venues of the best raves are thoughtfully provided on a BFBS programme that soldiers listen to. The programmes are fronted by a rave DJ called Steve Mason, who broadcasts for two hours at 8 pm on Wednesdays and 1 am on Saturdays. It is a programme also listened to by the Drugs Intelligence Teams.

There are other venues. As the cars fan out across the Continent on Friday afternoons, the betting is that some soldiers on leave are bound for the Pleasure Dome in Paderborn, or the Warehouse in Cologne, the Opera House in Hamburg, or the Park Zicht in Rotterdam. Others will make for the soft-drug havens of Holland; not just to Amsterdam, but to The Hague, Rotterdam, Arnhem and Eindhoven. Soldiers in Rheindahlen need only travel a few miles for their fix. Over the Dutch/German border is the small town of Venlo. In the coffee houses and along the banks of the River Maas, some seventy traffickers, many of them of Turkish origin, have set out their stalls.

Advocates of the soft line on soft drugs often argue that their decriminalization will lead to the elimination of the criminal element and a fall in prices, using as an analogy the outcome of the lifting of prohibition in America. That indeed is what has happened in Holland. Prices are lower, lower than in the criminalizing countries around them like France, Belgium and Britain. This fact has not escaped the notice of the sharper British soldier. In Holland he can buy drugs from between twenty and fifty per cent cheaper than the equivalent in Germany and Britain. He can make as much as £2,000 a trip, buying in Holland and either taking the drugs across the Channel to the UK or dealing on the camps with other British soldiers.

The British soldier has never been an angel, but there is something depressing about the current scenario. When the Army arrived in Germany in 1945 it was as a liberator-avenger. Idealism shone bright. It was a righteous war waged against an evil regime, and right had triumphed. Of nowhere was that more true than a huge military complex three hours' drive from Hamburg that the British call Hohne, the German police call 'Little England', and which before 1945 was known by a more chilling name – Belsen. The story of what has happened in Hohne/Belsen symbolizes what has happened in the soul of the British soldier, and perhaps in the soul of the nation from which he is recruited.

The development of this area into what it is today began in 1934, when the German Army faced rapid expansion due to universal conscription. A new training area was needed, where two divisions could train simultaneously. The sparsely populated Lüneberg Heath was chosen, and despite protest, Hitler ordered eleven villages to be evacuated to make way for a training area and two military camps, one at Hohne and one at Fallingbostel, comprising an area of about 200 square miles. The Wehrmacht soldiers billeted on these two camps received drilling and tank training on the twelve new ranges. The same soldiers later took part in the invasion of France, Poland and Russia.

The notorious concentration camp came into existence with the arrival of Russian prisoners-of-war in 1941. They were housed in the huts erected for the workmen on the Hohne and Fallingbostel camp projects. From them, the concentration of huts evolved into a full-scale concentration camp.

Belsen was not an extermination camp like Auschwitz, or a labour camp like Dachau. It was a special camp for prominent Jews, who were seen as useful hostages who could be ransomed, or exchanged for Germans interned abroad. To begin with, conditions were reasonably good as far as concentration camp conditions went. But matters deteriorated rapidly in 1944 as the Allied and Russian fronts began to close together. Concentration camps in the east were overrun. But, instead of handing over the prisoners to the advancing Allies, the Germans sent them to central collection points, of which Belsen was one.

In December 1944 there were 15,000 prisoners in the camp. By April 1945 there were 60,000 with 30,000 already dead of starvation, dysentery and typhus. One of those who died in Belsen was Anne Frank.

Belsen – (above) the RMP escort the Nazi guards into captivity; (below) the British Army burns the prison camp to the ground and takes over the German barracks in nearby Hohne.

As the sound of the British advance reached the ears of the SS guards, they tried to conceal 10,000 unburied corpses, but on 15 April 1945 the British liberated Belsen. At the same time Allied prisoners-of-war were freed at Fallingbostel camp. The story that followed is one of which the Army can forever be proud. It made the SS guards bury the prisoners they had murdered, said prayers over communal graves, tended and fed the living, forced prominent German civilians to witness the horrors on their own doorsteps, and handed the guilty over to justice. (Eleven senior SS personnel, including the Camp Commandant, Josef Kramer, were sentenced to death and hanged.) Then it torched Belsen. Only then was the Union Jack raised over the camp. 'The British flag does not fly over brutality, disgrace and murder, but after this camp is burnt, you will see the British flag, and you will know these horrors are over,' said the British officer in charge. A visitor to Belsen today will find twelve neat mounds containing 23,200 bodies.

Now that Belsen concentration camp was no more, the British brought the Jews into Hohne Camp. The Round House, used by the Germans as an officers' club and by British soldiers and their families today as a social centre, became a makeshift hospital. Those who were well were housed in the barrack blocks, awaiting emigration. They left from the very loading ramp on which they had arrived. The establishment of the state of Israel in 1948 hastened the process, but the last inmate of Belsen did not leave until September 1950.

As the Jews moved out, the victorious British troops moved in. Now there was a new threat from the east, and the tanks that rolled across France and

The SIB HQ at Hohne – once a German Army barrack block.

the low countries, across the Maas and the Rhine, were on the Hohne ranges, playing out war-games, fighting an imaginary war against the Red Army that everyone prayed would never happen. For over thirty years, regiments came and went, but there was a point and purpose to these exercises, as Harriers and Hunters swooped overhead, and Centurion tanks thundered across the great flat plain of northern Europe. There was nothing to stop the overwhelming numbers the Russians could put into the field; no great natural barriers. NATO thinking at that time was simply to hold the Russian might for a few crucial days, just long enough to prepare to unleash the nuclear deterrent on Russian cities. For a generation brought up to fear Russia and Soviet strength, what happened next was truly amazing. Years of *perestroika* under Secretary Gorbachev led to the dismantling of the Warsaw Pact. The climax was the destruction of the Berlin Wall in 1989.

In Europe there was a collective sigh of relief. But very soon it was realized that 'peace in our time' would have a profound effect on the services. To a government strapped for cash it was a godsend. There was now little need to maintain such a large standing Army. A series of management surveys followed in the early 1990s, each dignified by a reassuring name, although that fooled no one. In effect they were cost-cutting exercises. There was 'Front Line First', then there was 'Options for Change' followed by 'Drawdown'. The Treasury gnawed and nibbled and bit huge chunks out of the services. It would have been extraordinary if the Army had maintained its morale in the 1990s and gone whistling off to work.

As it was, into a system already reeling from its mauling at the hands of the politicians came a trickle of recruits from backgrounds where drug-abuse is almost a normal part of day-to-day existence. Today's eighteen- to twenty-five -year-olds do not recoil in horror at the idea of a joint or an Ecstasy tablet. They were also in Germany, home of the American serviceman, who was no stranger to drugs. In fact, so drug-calloused was he that he was now subject to compulsory random drug-testing, a course of action the British Army was to adopt in 1995.

Capt. Mal Heasman, a soft-spoken, somewhat retiring officer in the RMP, is in charge of Drugs Intelligence in Germany. The causes of the undermining of the British Army by drugs is, he says, 'bravado, peer-pressure, wanting to be one of the boys, a desire to experiment. Drugs are there; they're readily available. The soldier is in the right age group. Some have joined the Army from a drug environment in civilian life. And don't forget, you've got the people who are out there, quite willing to sell any controlled substance to anyone who's got the money. Soldiers have always got money.'

Mal Heasman is reluctant to put any figure on the number of soldiers

involved in drug-abuse. No one knows for sure, but educated guesses can be made, and figures bandied around in military circles suggest that in the eighteen to forty age group, which comprises ninety per cent of the Army, 1 in 4, or possibly as many as 2 in 5, will dabble in drugs in some form or another, from puffing on a cannabis cigarette once in a while at one end of the spectrum, to full-blown trafficking and dealing at the other. If these figures are anything near the truth, the Army has a horrific problem. The best hard evidence comes from the RMP's Central Criminal Records and Intelligence office based in London. In 1993, the total number of cases of drug offences investigated was 1,675.

Recognizing the seriousness of the situation, the Army has decided to introduce random drug-testing. It is persuaded that this measure has massively reduced drug-taking in the US Army, which once had even greater problems. Under the American system each soldier is expected to be tested randomly three times a year, but this would be far too costly for the British Treasury, and it remains to be seen how effective the new measure will be. In any case, as Capt. Heasman points out, random urine-testing will only identify the drug-users. It will not identify the drug supplier, against whose activities the main thrust of his energies is directed.

Nowhere is the thought that their soldiers may be drug-abusers more abhorrent than in those old regiments with a pride, a pedigree and a list of battle honours that bristle with some of the most resonant names in British military history; names like Waterloo, Blenheim, Balaclava. Such a regiment is the much-amalgamated Queen's Royal Hussars, based at Fallingbostel, and still, despite many absorptions and a rebirth under a new cap badge, a true aristocrat. The QRH has its own polo-ground; its officers' mess gleams with regimental silver portraying fierce moustachioed officers astride cavalry

Capt. Mal Heaseman, in charge of the Drugs Intelligence undercover teams through Germany.

chargers. About the walls are hung oil paintings of nineteenth-century battles painted in loving and bloodthirsty detail, but also, in more sentimental mood, a soft and attractive portrait of the young Princess Margaret.

To become an officer in the QRH is a privilege not given to all. It is not enough to hold the Queen's commission to become a Queen's Royal Hussar. A would-be second-lieutenant must first submit himself to the scrutiny of his brother officers. 'He comes and stays with us in the mess, so that he can look at us, and we can look at him. Quite honestly, if he's not the right sort, he simply wouldn't fit in. It is therefore better for all sides if he goes off somewhere else,' a languid subaltern informs us.

We are back in that world of officers-with-private-means, which is allied to an inbred instinct that informs a group whether he is, or is not, 'one of us'. One young man, who was 'one of us', nevertheless laboured under the crippling disadvantage of being christened 'Gary'. He was promptly, and without any say on his part, rechristened 'David'. He learned this soon after his acceptance when he could not find his place-name at the huge mess table. After wandering helplessly and in vain, he was finally ushered into his seat. It was only then that he learned he had been renamed. Another subaltern had a Fiat Uno. One day he found it had been destroyed. His brother officers then clubbed together to buy him something more in keeping with the reputation of the regiment.

That soldiers from an élite outfit like the QRH could be infected, contaminated in the grubby, murky world of drugs is truly appalling. The two are surely incompatible. The regiment's CO, Lt. Col. Nigel Beer, thought the unthinkable. He is a realist, although there is hurt behind his eyes as he talks of 'a drug sub-culture', 'a secondary mafia', 'a drug-crime welfare existing in a family' and the utter incompatibility of drug-abuse and soldiering.

Nigel Beer has brought into being a number of practical measures against drug-abusers in his regiment. First, no one tainted by involvement in drugs will be allowed near armoured vehicles, trucks or weapons. That being so, the soldier is effectively debarred from normal regimental duties, and ends up doing fairly menial tasks like sweeping, or weeding the paths and flowerbeds in the predominantly garden camp compound of Fallingbostel.

Secondly, while awaiting court martial, which can take six months or more, drug-abusers are segregated from the other soldiers into a sort of purdah, isolated barrack-room accommodation, where they are under strict supervision. 'Thirdly', Nigel Beers says, 'I remove their regimental cap badge, to make it quite clear to everyone that this is conduct unacceptable to members of this regiment, and they are not fit to be seen as members of the regiment. By that sort of measure, I hope we can send out a clear message to the young, impressionable soldier that drug-taking is not a streetwise, macho thing to do. It's a loser's game, and it is incompatible with being a member of this regiment, and a member of the British Army.'

The CO has a formidable array of legal options open to him against a soldier drug-abuser in his regiment. Normally the man will face a court martial. If the offence is serious he may spend years in prison. If the sentence is for over two years, it will be in a civilian prison, while a sentence of two years or less will be served in the Army's own prison, the Military Corrective Training Centre, known as the 'Glasshouse', in Colchester, and followed by a discharge from the Army. If, on the other hand, the soldier has experimented briefly, and not attempted to involve others, the CO can recommend that he is retained in the Army, although some weeks or months may be served in the Glasshouse.

There is a further alternative, open uniquely to servicemen, but not to other citizens of the realm. It is known as an AGAI 5 – short for Army General Administrative Instruction number 5. The fact that it exists at all is an indication of the serious nature of the drug-taking problem in the Army.

There is a SIB saying: 'The Friday afternoon nous.' 'You see,' they say, 'something always happens on Friday afternoon, just when we're all getting ready for the weekend.' It is extraordinary how often this is the case. It was on Friday afternoon that Signalman Brown (as we will call him) was standing confused and crestfallen as Cpl Martin on attachment with the Hohne SIB intoned the familiar mantra: 'I am arresting you under Section 74 of the Army Act 1955, as I suspect you have been involved in the misuse of controlled drugs. You don't have to say anything unless you wish to do so, but what you say may be given in evidence.'

Signalman Brown had surrendered himself to the medical officer under the AGAI 5 procedure. Under this instruction, if a soldier comes forward and voluntarily admits to drug-abuse, he is not punished. Providing he cooperates with the RMP, giving them the names of other soldiers he knows to be taking drugs, he is given a discharge from the Army, and he is not prosecuted.

But Signalman Brown still had to submit himself to a body search, which is not as drastic as it sounds. No human orifice is explored; a doctor would have to be present were that to happen. A suspect strips to his underpants, and his divested clothes are the subject of minute scrutiny. After that, his room and his car are searched, first with a sniffer dog, and then by the two SIB investigators. Although the AGAI 5 was designed to rid the Army of its rotten apples with the minimum of fuss, soldiers were quick to realize that it could also provide them with an easy and less expensive way of getting out of the Army, so there are still hurdles for the soldier to overcome. The AGAI 5 is not a complete doddle. If, in the searches that follow, drugs, even in small quantities, are found, the discharge can be deemed null and void, and the Army can come down on the man with the full vigour of the Manual of Military Law.

No one, however innocent, enjoys being searched. As Signalman Brown looked anxiously on, two men and a dog pored and pawed over his belongings. Anything could come to light at such a time, whether relevant to the enquiry in hand or not: stolen property, barrack room theft being one of the curses of army life; a compromising letter from a gay lover, all homosexual relationships being viewed askance by the authorities. Anything that the search team finds

Capt Wooldridge's 'Fighting Seventieth' in Germany. Eleven detectives plus interpreters, secretaries and 'Buddy'.

Cpl Steve Graham-dog. If the urine analysis proves positive, Buddy will get an extra gravy dinner.

can form the basis of different charges. And since the privates in Hohne and Fallingbostel tend to share their rooms with another soldier, that absent soldier, against whom no charges have been brought, is equally vulnerable. Especially as Buddy is rampaging around with little regard for the name of the soldier on the charge sheet.

'Buddy' is a three-year-old brown and white cocker spaniel. His handler is Cpl Steve Graham. There is another Cpl Steve Graham attached to the SIB at Hohne. To avoid confusion the first Steve Graham is called Steve Graham-dog, the second Steve Graham-no-dog. Steve Graham-dog adores Buddy. He takes intense personal pleasure in Buddy's successes, and rewards him accordingly with extra gravy dinners. He suspects that the officer commanding the SIB section, Capt. John Wooldridge, has his doubts about Buddy, and wonders whether in terms of drugs hauls sniffed out Buddy really earns his keep. That is why Steve Graham-dog has an I-told-you-so-expression on his face whenever Buddy finds drugs. He would not, as corporal to captain, express those convictions any other way, but if Steve Graham-dog had a tail, he would wag it at such times.

Buddy has the rank of private, and his own regimental number, 8087, tattooed on his left ear. Steve Graham-dog is often asked whether the sniffer dogs are addicted to the substances they find. 'Emphatically not,' is his reply. To Buddy the search is a game he has played many times with his handler in training sessions, when a parcel containing a drug is hidden in a room, and Buddy is let off the leash to search for it. The searching is punctuated throughout by Steve Graham's encouragement: 'Go on boy . . . search . . . good boy . . . good boy . . .'

Buddy found nothing in Signalman Brown's room nor in the nearby ablution block. But when he was introduced to the soldier's car, his tail began to wag excitedly and he began to paw at the upholstery of the back seat. When this was removed, a small amount of what looked like cannabis resin was recovered, later confirmed when it was tested in the Scenes of Crime room. It was Buddy's fifteenth strike.

Signalman Brown would get his discharge, but not the painless discharge prescribed in the AGAI 5 procedure. And when, in the following week, he was found with twenty-five Ecstasy tablets, his fate was sealed. But it is not the Signalman Browns that are the Army's prime concern. They are small fry. What the Army is after are the traffickers and dealers in their midst.

To combat these, in 1985 the RMP set up special operations units in Britain and abroad called DITs, Drugs Intelligence Teams. These are made up of hand-picked young men and women who, in a corps noted for its impeccable military turnout, would cause apoplexy in the regimental sergeant major because of their quite deliberate outrageous appearance. Punk hairdos on the girls, with rings in their noses, and slashed jeans, the boys perhaps in loud bermudas and back-to-front baseball caps bearing maybe a cannabis motif. Less soldierly-looking soldiers would be impossible to find.

In Britain, there are eight DIT operators, junior NCOs under the command of Capt. Joanne Naylor. They work the pubs, discos and raves covertly. They all live together in a safe house in the Didcot area near Oxford, and their 'life' as a DIT operative lasts no more than a year. Beyond that time their identity could not be protected with certainty. Theirs is a dangerous job. In attempting to get close to the main players in the drugs trade, they run some risk of involvement with people who would not hesitate to use firearms. DIT teams tend to work at weekends, when places of entertainment are busy. They look like youngsters on the town out for a good time. Inside the discos they move around, chatting, smiling, dancing, getting to know people, watching and noting the suppliers. They have a special dispensation to smoke cannabis themselves.

Capt. Naylor's job in Germany is performed by the aforementioned Capt. Mal Heasman. In one sense his job is more clear-cut, due to the special circumstances of working in a foreign land. Jurisdiction over British servicemen and their dependants is in the hands of the RMP. This is not the case at home, where off base, the civil police have jurisdiction. But in another sense Heasman's job is more complex. His mandate extends only up to the German border. When soldiers misbehave in France and Holland, Heasman cannot officially send his operatives across the borders in pursuit of them, without the cooperation of the host nation police and judicial authorities.

The DIT teams are at the behest of SIB units, who may have need of their specialist services. That was why the DIT team spent much of October 1994 in Hohne Camp. Operation Paternal was an attempt by 70th Section of the SIB to take out a soldier suspected of drug-dealing from his married quarters. In charge of that operation was the officer commanding 70th Section, Capt. John Wooldridge. The targeted soldier was a lance corporal in the Queen's Royal Hussars, whose CO, Lt. Col. Nigel Beer, was determined to root out drug-abuse from among his men. Throughout Operation Paternal there was the closest cooperation between Beer and Wooldridge, the former a high-flyer in command of a blue-chip regiment, the latter a blunt-speaking Hampshire man with a redeeming sense of humour, who had risen from the non-commissioned ranks to become an officer and OC (officer commanding) of the Special Investigation Branch in Hohne Camp.

Over a period of weeks and months the SIB had been building up a scenario that suggested that in the sister camps at Fallingbostel, half

Cpl Steve Graham-dog, plus Buddy, on the scent.

an hour's drive across the military ranges, there was evidence of drug-abuse. The evidence came from soldiers themselves, many of whom dislike the presence of drugs in their midst, and also from drug-abusers themselves, soldiers on AGAI 5 discharges, who are cooperating with the RMP. Evidence also came from soldiers arrested for drug-abuse who are routinely asked in RMP interviews to name names.

Suspicion fell on LCpl Fisher (as we will call him), married with two young children, and living in married quarters on the periphery of Fallingbostel Camp. Weekend parties were often held in these quarters. Soldiers were seen to arrive, stay for a brief time, and then leave. The Wild Boar NAAFI at Fallingbostel also fell under suspicion. There was evidence of soldiers from the Queen's Royal Hussars and the Royal Highland Fusiliers openly smoking cannabis on the premises.

It was decided to advance on both fronts. A DIT-trained girl would be found employment in the NAAFI and supplied with the necessary false documentation. She would also be given a special Army dispensation to smoke cannabis, if the need arose. Secondly, the full DIT team should be brought up from its base in Rheindahlen to mount a round-the-clock surveillance of Fisher's married quarters.

It was at this point that Wooldridge faced his first difficulty. He needed an empty married quarters overlooking Fisher's house into which the surveillance team could be introduced. There was no such house.

But this was QRH territory. Lines between the SIB and the QRH adjutant's office were busy. Overlooking Fisher's quarters about fifty yards away across a grassed area was a similiar block, two storeys high, containing four married quarters in all, two above and two below. Any one of these four flats would be ideal.

The QRH agree to Wooldridge's request to get one of these families off the scene by inventing a bereavement that would justify three weeks' compassionate leave back in the UK. Cpl Steve Graham-dog is delegated with the job of telling the soldier that he can expect three weeks unexpected holiday. It happens that the soldier in question has been cultivated by Graham, and from his vantage-point has been a prime source of information on the suspicious comings and goings to Fisher's quarters. But he is naturally anxious that his anonymity and that of his wife, be preserved. Graham reassures him. Then the soldier's wife begins to express fears that a three-week absence may mean she will lose her job. Jobs for women around the military bases are at a premium and eagerly sought. There is an inexhaustable pool of labour from which the NAAFIs and YMCAs can recruit.

In addition, Capt. Wooldridge is beginning to have doubts about the wisdom of this plan. It will be impossible to confine it to the CO and Adjutant of the QRH. Clerks in the Company Office will become involved, the men who fill out the leave passes and the travel warrants. All regiments are rife with gossip. Word will spread. It may reach the ears of Fisher himself. From a security point of view the plan is as leaky as a sieve.

It was then, quite by chance, that the SIB heard that one of the other four flats in the block overlooking Fisher's would become vacant soon. A soldier and his family were being posted elsewhere a fortnight later. It was a straightforward matter to arrange that the married quarters should remain untenanted for at least three weeks after the family's departure.

So it was finally that at 4 am one autumn morning two figures let themselves into the empty married quarters directly opposite the suspect's home. They chose a time when the street lighting was off, and there was very little chance of being spotted by pedestrians or passing cars. They made several journeys to the waiting car in the car park at the back and away from Fisher's quarters, carrying some boxes of technical gear and a few personal belongings. At a whispered signal the car sped off.

19,750 Ecstasy tablets – the largest drug haul to date recovered from a serving British soldier. Estimated street value: £400,000.

It was the dead of night, but the two drug operatives could not turn on any lights. Scufflings, doors opening and closing, conversations, radios, lights going on and off, all this could give their presence away. Sound insulation in modern housing is poor, and it is even poorer when that house is completely devoid of all furniture. Fortunately for the DIT team the floors were carpeted, and there were curtains.

Groping their way down the hall, the two men found a living-room, unrolled their sleeping bags and waited for the dawn. So began nearly three weeks watching and waiting. Conversations were whispered. To relieve the tedium, listening to music was possible, but only on earphones. No taps could be turned on, lest the noise of a filling water tank aroused the suspicions of those around. The lavatory bowl could not be flushed. Such was the need for silence, such were the acoustics in an empty flat, that urine had to be directed against the porcelain of the lavatory to deaden a noise that could sound like a sudden waterfall. To manage this in a pitch-black bathroom was particularly difficult. Accordingly, the surveillance team found it beneficial to limit its liquid intake. Defecation was even worse. Since the flush could not be used, for hygienic and aesthetic reasons the team were required to adopt a squatting position and defecate into white plastic bags. At the end of a shift, some thirty-six or forty-eight hours later, their gruesome takeaways would be removed from the scene of operations and disposed of. Shifts always changed at four in the morning.

The nights were always the worst. Dusk comes early in October. From about six at night to six in the morning the team sat in darkness with the minimum of comfort – no chairs, no tables, no camp beds, unable to use the lights, unable to use the cooking facilities, living off stale sandwiches, crisps and chocolates.

The house from which they watched was unlikely to attract any attention from passers-by. It seemed an ordinary ground-floor flat with its curtains drawn, like the other flats in the block, but there was one difference. The windows of the other flats were hung with net curtains. This flat had double white curtains with coloured blobs and they were very slightly apart. Only a

Capt. (now Major) John Wooldridge, officer commanding the SIB in Aldershot, home of the British Army, and – of considerable interest to the RMP – home-depot of the much-feared Parachute Regiment.

very observant passer-by would notice – and he would have to come right up to the window itself – that set back a foot or so from the chink in the curtains was a video camera.

Inside, one of the DIT team lies or sits on the floor. Before him lies an official log. Connected to the video camera is a monitor TV. The camera is focused on the communal door to Fisher's flat. Every coming, and every going, of man, woman, tradesman or child is logged, with description and time. A video recorder is on time-lapse record. A copy of the tape goes down to Rheindahlen, where analysts compare faces with their own rogues gallery. There is also a radio telephone. The team is in touch with Capt. Wooldridge and his RSM, Terry Burrough. They can brief them on the latest development and receive fresh instructions. They can also talk on it to the RMP data bank, which will tell them the owner of any car seen cruising or parking near Fisher's quarters, provided the car is owned by a soldier. It sounds efficient enough, but it is not. The video camera cannot record in the dark, neither can the human eye see. The night-sight lenses are on the blink. It means that for almost half the time the DIT team is in situ – and at the very time when drug-related activity is assumed to take place – there can be no real surveillance at all. They are literally working in the dark.

After a fortnight of patient and uncomfortable logging, the DIT team was close to despair. LCpl Fisher's behaviour was impeccable. During the week he left promptly, ostensibly to go to his job in the QRH stores. He returned at

After the arrest of Fisher at the border, the RMP are called to collect his abandoned car. It was then taken away for detailed forensic examination.

approximately five o'clock. Others in the block left and returned at blameless hours. There were no parties, no suspicious visitors, no 'special' knocks at the door. Despite every effort to conceal Operation Paternal, it was as if someone, somewhere had tipped Fisher the wink that they were on to him. The only detail in the pattern that seemed in any way out of the ordinary was the fact that for two Saturdays in succession Fisher had gone out at 3 pm and had not returned until the early hours of the next day. That much could be seen in the dark. Fisher had driven his red Honda CRX, in itself a surprising car for a lance corporal to own, especially as it had been bought for cash the previous month.

Meanwhile, there were some grounds for guarded optimism regarding the girl who had infiltrated the Wild Boar NAAFI. She had been invited to a party and had accepted. Sooner or later, it was felt, the joints might be passed around.

Back in Hohne, Wooldridge and Burrough decided that the DIT surveillance would not go on indefinitely. Theirs was not the only operation in Germany in urgent need of its experience. Since the only mysterious aspect of Fisher's behaviour was his Saturday disappearances, they decided that on the next Saturday they would follow Fisher from his married quarters to wherever he was going, and arrest him as he left the autobahn on his way home. The Operation was rechristened 'Operation Paternal – Take That'. ('A nice touch that,' the RSM thought. He had teenage daughters.) The DIT team reinforced by the SIB investigators were to meet at 1 pm at the safe house.

The safe house was a pleasant detached house on the outskirts of the attractive little market town of Celle, where most of the SIB themselves live in married quarters. It had been recently acquired as a rape victim crisis centre, fully equipped as a working home where molested wives or children could stay in peace and safety while their problems were attended to. (There were thirty-seven cases of child abuse in the Army worldwide in 1993, the latest year for which there are figures.) But in the absence of rape victims, or abused children, the safe house was a perfect refuge for off-duty DIT operatives recuperating after a forty-eight-hour shift watching the comings and goings of LCpl Fisher from the OP (Observation Point).

They all met at the appointed hour, but there was some ominously bad news. The surveillance team telephoned to say that the bird had flown; just minutes before 'Operation Paternal – Take That' was about to start, Fisher was seen leaving his quarters, much earlier than usual. He was carrying a white ironed shirt on a hanger, and a black hold-all. He syphoned some petrol from his second-best car into the Honda CRX, and then he drove off.

The feeling of disappointment in the safe house was palpable. By now Fisher could be anywhere, *en route* for any one of half a dozen countries. Nevertheless, four cars set off for Fallingbostel, while Capt. Wooldridge stayed behind in an ops rooms in Hohne, accompanied by his interpreter, Mrs Holz.

It was 3 pm. If the pattern established over the two previous Saturdays was to hold, Fisher would not return until the early hours. As the cars took up their positions in and around the Fallingbostel Camp, their occupants knew they were in for a long and possibly pointless vigil. Meanwhile, back in his ops room at Hohne, Capt. Wooldridge tried to limit the damage caused by the decision to mount the operation too late; had it begun an hour earlier they might well have had Fisher in their sights.

Through Mrs Holz, the German police at Hamburg, Hanover and Bremen were given details of the Red Honda CRX, as were the border police at Bad Bentheim. Wooldridge put a call through to the guardroom of the QRH and asked to speak to a sergeant major known to him, and known to be on duty that night. Would he do Wooldridge a favour? Would he ring Fisher's wife and ask to speak to Fisher on some regimental business – perhaps regarding a bunch of keys that was lost, or on any other plausible matter? Naturally, Mrs Fisher would say that her husband was not at home, in which case the sergeant major should ask her when he would be back. The sergeant major agreed to help Wooldridge. Half an hour later he was back in touch. He described Mrs Fisher as 'very cagey'. She told him that she had no idea where her husband was, that he had left with another man and would not be back until the early hours.

On hearing this, Wooldridge suspended the operation, and all cars returned to Hohne. Everyone was made aware of the situation and given half an hour to get something warm to eat. Then, at 9 pm, they were back again on station, redeployed at four different vantage-points in the vicinity of the Fishers' married quarters. On a day when almost everything had gone wrong, they clung to the one certainty, that sooner or later, Fisher would *have* to come home, wouldn't he?

The hours passed. The dead of night turned to a pale dawn. Still no sign of Fisher. There was the beginning of stubble on chins. Eyes were bleary, legs cramped. Careful though each man was on his liquid intake, no one could leave his car to urinate.

It was not so long ago that the IRA had mounted a campaign against British Forces in Germany. All those lectures urging soldiers to be observant and report anything unusual now began to tell against the DIT team and the SIB, who had been sitting for hours in four parked cars. What was going on? The RMP

police stations at Hohne and Fallingbostel received several calls from soldiers and soldiers' families not used to seeing cars full of silent unshaven men in civilian clothes staring out of the window for hours on end on a Sunday morning. They must be up to some mischief.

Sunday morning passed. It was at about three in the afternoon, twenty-six hours after the start of 'Operation Paternal – Take That', that call sign Romeo asked all cars to listen in. Terry Burrough, the RSM gave the order 'Endex, endex'. Wearily the convoy returned to Hohne for a debriefing.

Three weeks' surveillance from the empty married quarters, twenty-six

Surveillance operation mounted from an empty married quarter in Fallingbostel. (Video camera concealed behind curtains of window, lower picture, bottom row, centre.)

hours sitting wretchedly in cars, watching and waiting, had all been in vain. 'It's been miserable, boring and thankless, and I'm as disappointed as you are,' said Wooldridge to his dispirited men. 'But the one good thing that has come out of all this is that this is the third Saturday on the trot that he's been away. He's up to something, and in the next two or three weeks we will mount the same operation again. Drive carefully. Thanks a lot, lads.'

No one really believed they would try again in a hurry. Despite their extreme fatigue and the injunction to drive carefully, the car park emptied in an instant. Everyone wanted to get home for what was left of a miserable weekend. To compound the agony, the DIT girl planted in the NAAFI reported that her party had been an entirely innocuous affair.

As for LCpl Fisher, he did return. Indeed he had to return. It was at 8 pm, five hours after Operational Paternal was aborted, that the red Honda CRX returned to the married quarters, leaving a lay observer to wonder why, having expended all that time and effort, the SIB and DIT did not go that extra mile, knowing that they were on to a certainty.

The border between Germany and Holland appears to be entirely unmanned. Customs sheds and passport controls are forlornly empty as traffic speeds by in both directions. But there is a discreet eye on movements somewhere. At 1 am on the Thursday after Operation Paternal was called off, the red Honda CRX was stopped by German border police, following the tip-off from Wooldridge at the weekend. Inside was LCpl Fisher and another soldier. In their possession was a small quantity of cannabis resin and cocaine, and in the boot were four tupperware jars filled with tablets. The German police alerted the nearest RMP Special Investigation Unit, which happened to be at Osnabrück. Fisher was arrested and charged in the first instance with being in possession of cocaine and cannabis resin. He was locked up in his regimental guardroom at Fallingbostel, while enquiries continued.

The plastic containers were sent to the Government Laboratories at Teddington, which confirmed that the tablets were indeed Ecstasy. There were 19,750, with a street value of £400,000. This was to date the largest drug haul ever discovered on a single British soldier.

Wooldridge and his men were rightly pleased that their target was indeed all they had suspected, although that pleasure would have been heightened had they personally made the arrest. Fisher has said very little. It is known that the drugs were obtained from a man in Amsterdam, but no one knows if Fisher is a big fish or a minnow, whether he purchased the Ecstasy himself for sale, at a huge profit, to British soldiers, or whether he was simply a courier. Whatever the truth of the matter, Capt. Wooldridge commented that he found it disturbing that a British soldier could be so trusted by major drug barons that he was thought suited to carry such a huge consignment.

If found guilty, Fisher will probably receive a sentence of some years in a civilian gaol. But what happens to the wives and children of convicted soldiers? As in civilian life, they are often the real victims. A soldier's family lives in a 'tied cottage', called married quarters. Once convicted, a soldier's pay stops, and the wife is given ninety-one days by the Army to find alternative accommodation, alternative schooling for her children, an alternative life. The penalties are indeed daunting, but who dares say that we have seen the last of a British soldier trying to carry out a major drugs coup?

CHAPTER 6

CAKE TINS FOR KOHIMA

They came for Purcell at about 9.30 in the morning, just as the kitchen staff were clearing up after breakfast. There were three of them: SSgt Howard Wright, with Cpl Higgins in attendance, and Maj. Wood to act as a silent witness. Purcell led the way from the cookhouse to his office in an annexe behind the main kitchens.

'Would you take a seat, sir?' said Wright with an icy friendliness.

Purcell had gone very white. He was trembling slightly. If it is true that at certain turning-points in life there is a moment of terrible clarity that reveals what the future may hold, then that moment had come in the life of Malcolm Purcell. Married with three children, Purcell is nearing the end of twenty-two years' unblemished service in the Army as a warrant officer class 2, and looking forward to a second career outside the Army with gratuities and a pension. (To those unfamiliar with Army ranks, a WO2 is high up the scale of non-commissioned officers; the rank structure is as follows: lance corporal, corporal, sergeant, staff sergeant, warrant officer class 2, warrant

Catterick Court Martial Centre. The Judge Advocate sits in the centre, flanked by officers who decide the verdict and the sentence.

officer class 1. The penultimate rank is commonly known as 'sergeant major', and the top rank as 'regimental sergeant major'.)

'Are you 24240165 M.J. Purcell?'

'Yes.'

'What's your actual appointment here, sir?' A slight emphasis on the 'sir' made it sound almost insolent.

'Regimental Messing Officer.'

'Right, sir. I'm S/Sgt Wright of the Royal Military Police Special Investigation Branch. I'm arresting you under section 74 of the Army Act because I have reason to believe you have been involved in false

MEMBER

JUDGE ADVOCATE GENERAL

accounting. You do not have to say anything unless you wish to do so, but what you say . . .'

The time-honoured formula. Purcell says nothing.

'What I'd like to do now is carry out a search of this office for evidence which may support those charges.'

About an hour later the arrested man is escorted to the SIB for a taped interview under caution. SSgt Wright is carrying folders and account books seized from Purcell's filing cabinet. No one knows yet if this is a major fraud or a minor fiddle. It hardly matters. Purcell is in deep trouble. The Army will be merciless to any middle-manager in a responsible position found guilty of the most minor theft.

Hour by hour, day by day, the case against Purcell hardens. But to understand what may have happened, S/Sgt Wright of the SIB is going to have to immerse himself in CATPAC, the Army's computerized catering system. With regional variations, CATPAC lays down what soldiers will eat in their cookhouses on a menu cycle that changes daily but repeats every fourteen days. Put simply, 'if it's Thursday it must be steak and kidney pudding', although that is a travesty of the system, which holds out an extensive choice unheard of in the Army of old. The ingredients of this extensive choice are supplied by local dealers authorized by the Army. Their bills are submitted at the end of the month and paid by cheque from the public purse. This is called the 'Imprested Account'. But if there are emergencies, if for example ingredients run out, if some event is due to take place that is not part of the CATPAC meal cycle, there is a petty cash float called the 'extra messing fund'. It was this account that was in the control of the sergeant major and it was this account which found itself down by well over £400.

To get an advance from this float, the sergeant major would have to go to the office of Mrs Maureen White, who is a service fund accountant. On receiving the money from Mrs White, he would sign a receipt, which remains in her cash box, until the advance is cleared by an invoice to show that the money has been spent legitimately. Once she has got this invoice, Mrs White will hand back the sergeant major's signed receipt, which he destroys in her presence to show that the transaction is complete.

But Mrs White has not been at all happy about the way that the fund has been used. Her suspicions were first aroused when the sergeant major rushed in one day and asked for a £30 advance to buy 'cake tins for Kohima'. (Every year the veterans of the Battle of Kohima, 1944, are entertained over a summer weekend at Imphal Barracks, York.) Two days later he borrowed another £20. Mrs White expected an invoice for cake tins from one of the city's suppliers of kitchen accessories to be returned in due course. But the

Kohima veterans celebrate the fiftieth anniversary of the battle, at Imphal Barracks, York.

receipt, when it came back, was not for cake tins, it was for fruit and vegetables. From that moment Mrs White subjected the sergeant major's request for cash advances to a minute scrutiny. One bill for £62.65 from L.F. West particularly caught her eye. This was a genuine invoice, and the sergeant major had been paid £62.65 against it. But Mrs White knew that L.F. West was an authorized dealer, who would automatically be reimbursed the £62.65 through the 'Imprest Account' – the public purse – at the end of the month. In other words, the Army had paid twice for the same goods, once from the 'Imprest Account', and once through the 'extra messing account', apparently into the sergeant major's pocket.

When SSgt Wright visited Mrs White, she produced a number of such invoices all submitted over a period of three months. 'I suppose it was a culmination of things. Dates didn't tally on invoices, bills weren't raised, originals that had been paid were produced again, functions that goods had been purchased for were for wrong dates. It just didn't add up.'

It was time to call the sergeant major into SIB headquarters to give his explanation of the anomalies. In the long interview that followed, the sergeant major did not dispute that he submitted phony receipts, but he said that he had not pocketed the money himself. The money had been spent on provisions that he needed for the kitchen. He could not prove that this was so, because by now all the provisions that he had bought had been eaten. Every time SSgt Wright produced false receipts, or genuine receipts that had already been paid, the sergeant major said the same, that, yes, the receipts had been put in to satisfy the system, but that he had genuinely spent the money on the needs of the kitchen, and that, as far as he was concerned, was how he had been taught to use the 'extra messing account', and so had many others.

'At the end of the day, sergeant major,' said SSgt Wright, 'I must admit that I don't believe one word of what you are saying. I believe you have misused the system. You have produced receipts for whatever source to finance yourself.'

'No.'

'It's not just one little receipt which we can explain away. We are talking about a number of instances where exactly the same thing has happened time and time again. You go into the Pay Office and say, hand on heart, "I have purchased these items from the extra messing fund." Then, lo and behold, at the end of the day there is absolutely no evidence to support your claims that you did actually go out and buy those goods. You can't produce any paperwork to say "they went on the shelves there." It just can't be done.'

But the sergeant major put up a spirited defence: 'That was the way I was taught. That is the way I've been shown how to do it. I buy things for the kitchen, and obviously the money is not going to come back because I cannot take money out of the account [the Imprest Account] to pay into extra messing . . . But the money *is* put back through a percentage of the bills we raise from our customers at functions like coffee mornings, or corporals' mess buffets.'

At the end of the interview the sergeant major is told that there is sufficient evidence to justify disciplinary action being taken against him for theft, false accounting and forgery. But SSgt Wright does not feel confident. To prove theft, he has to prove dishonesty and the fact that the sergeant major has gained. He can do neither. In a perplexed frame of mind, he walks across the barracks to the building that houses Army Legal to get some advice from Capt. Susan Ridge.

SSGT WRIGHT: My own personal opinion of it is that without a doubt he has had his hand in the till but he has come up with the scenario that is going to be extremely difficult if not impossible to disprove.

CAPT. RIDGE: Except for the fact that he has changed his story in interview [the Sgt Maj was interviewed twice, and there were variations in detail between the two interviews].

SSGT WRIGHT: Yes, exactly. He has tied himself somewhat in knots and changed his own story which to my mind proves that he has been dishonest. Whether that will suffice for your purposes and the jury's purposes is another matter.

CAPT. RIDGE: I think it is somewhat borderline, isn't it? I take it you asked him, 'Did he consider that his actions were dishonest?' How does he come across to that type of questioning?

SSGT WRIGHT: As far as he is concerned, he believes that the system can be used that way.

CAPT. RIDGE: Right, so if he believes the system can be used that way, he doesn't think he has done anything dishonest?

SSGT WRIGHT: No.

CAPT. RIDGE: That is a great help! Because otherwise we come down to small offences like 'tampering with an official document'. A military offence.

SSGT WRIGHT: What we need to do together is decide whether it is worth going the whole hog for the heavier offences or whether we should cut our losses and go for something which we can prove.

CAPT. RIDGE: I must say it seems incredible that he could think that he could swap funds around, which is what he seems to be doing.

SSGT WRIGHT: That is what he is saying he is doing. I mean to my mind, I have sat across from the guy for a couple of hours, and I am quite happy in my own mind that he knows exactly what he has been doing, but he has come up with a clever answer for it, and one which is minimizing the damage to him, i.e. a military offence, without the stigma of a criminal record.

CAPT. RIDGE: Let's see . . . if we can do him on a dishonesty offence, he would probably have to go to a court martial and, if he was convicted of a theft offence, then because he is in a position of trust, he is looking at a prison sentence.

SSGT WRIGHT: Basically they would crucify him.

CAPT. RIDGE: Yes, he is looking at a prison sentence, rather than Colchester [the Army's own military corrective centre]. Yes, it is a big difference to him, isn't it?

SSGT WRIGHT: He mustn't get away with it.

CAPT. RIDGE: We will have a think and see what comes back.

SSGT WRIGHT: All right, ma'am, thanks for that.

All the services are very hard on servicemen in positions of responsibility who are suspected of dishonesty. The sergeant major's crime – if crime it was – was trivial. He is accused of fiddling about £450. If he were a chef in a big London Hotel, he would probably be shown the door, and given a reasonable reference. Not so the services. They pursue their errant middle-managers with vengeful ferocity. It will have been no consolation to the sergeant major to read early in 1995 that a petty officer (his equivalent rank in the Navy) was fined a colossal £17,000 for fiddling just £193. The petty officer was in fact grateful to the court martial. 'If it had been a magistrates court I would only have been fined about £150,' he said. What he feared was the loss of his redundancy package of more than £54,000. And that is what is uppermost in the sergeant major's mind: he is hoping to leave the Army soon with a cash sum of about £60,000, with which he plans to buy a pub. Now he could lose everything.

By now the Redcaps have prepared their dossier on the case and distributed it to, among others, the Army Legal Service, the equivalent of the Crown Prosecution Service. Col. Dick Austin and Capt. Susan Ridge have to decide whether to advise court martial, and, if so, what kind. Different courts martial can do different things to different ranks.

The first question to be resolved is whether a court martial can be justified.

CAPT. RIDGE: I think the problem is, and has been really all along, to what extent we can show that he was dishonest, and whether there is sufficient evidence that he was dishonest.

COL. AUSTIN: Yes, there's not much point taking this to court martial if he has just been stupid.

CAPT. RIDGE: Now, the SIB have come up with a number of statements. There's a statement from the service fund accountant, the rations clerk, and an NCO in the kitchen, all of whom say that the system is set up in such a way that the Master Chef has used the system wrongly. It shouldn't have happened.

COL. AUSTIN: Right, now are they talking reality or are they talking how the system should be?

CAPT. RIDGE: That's the danger. I think as it stands at the moment, if what they are talking is the reality, there is probably a good chance that we could show that the Master Chef may have been dishonest ...

COL. AUSTIN: Is this a dishonest

(Above) Chefs busy at work in the kitchens of Imphal Barracks.

(Below) CATPAC. A choice of dishes available for one day – a startling comparison with the cookhouses of old.

man or is this a man who is being stupid?

CAPT. RIDGE: I think it's a dishonest man if you go on the basis of what is said by Mrs White, the rations clerk and the NCO in the kitchen. If they were to be as firm in court as they are in their statements, then I think they could show that there are sufficient inconsistencies in his evidence to show that he was dishonest.

COL. AUSTIN: Right.

CAPT. RIDGE: If, however, they did not come up to proof, then I think it would be more difficult.

COL. AUSTIN: Quite, but we are assuming everyone comes up to proof, and one has to do that anyway. Unless there's any good reason why they shouldn't, then there is a more than fifty per cent chance of him being convicted of an offence of dishonesty. Is that about what you think?

CAPT. RIDGE: I would hope so.

So with an element of doubt apparent in the minds of both legal officers, there is agreement that there are grounds for a court martial. The choice is between a District Court Martial or a General Court Martial. Tacitly the two legal officers believe the sergeant major must be dealt with severely. That would rule out a District Court Martial, which cannot sentence a warrant officer to a term of imprisonment.

CAPT. RIDGE: I was thinking in my advice letter of probably recommending General Court Martial.

COL. AUSTIN: Obviously, if it's not a General Court Martial, he can't be locked up or kicked out, if that's what the Court thinks is the right way of dealing with him. District Court Martial on the other hand can reduce him in rank and fine him. Obviously, it's quite a severe penalty to reduce him in rank from warrant officer down to private.

CAPT. RIDGE: The 'extra messing fund' is actually down they reckon about £440. It's not a great deal of money . . . but having said that, as you say, he is a WO2 and he is in a fiduciary position.

Capt. Ridge puts it in a nutshell. Malcolm Purcell is a sergeant major in a position of trust. Rank and responsibility, if abused, bring down serious consequences.

CAPT. RIDGE: It's not a very large account, but he has only had it in his control for about three months .   . .

COL AUSTIN: Hmmm, there is no doubt about it, if he's been dishonest, he breached people's trust, and we don't need warrant officers of that type and certainly I wouldn't lose any sleep if he got locked up. But one needs to make sure that these things are treated fairly.

CAPT. RIDGE: I have to say my experience of recent possible courts martial of this type are that they've been locked up.

COL. AUSTIN: Yes, indeed, which points one towards saying it should be a General Court Martial because why should a warrant officer . . . be treated more leniently?

CAPT. RIDGE: Exactly.

COL. AUSTIN: And I certainly go along with that. The higher you are, the harder you fall.

Accordingly, the advice from the Army Legal Service is that the sergeant major be brought before a General Court Martial. The letter is despatched to the sergeant major's CO, Lt. Col. Andrew Forster, who agrees that the matter should go for trial.

After analysing all the evidence, six charges of theft are formulated, adding up to a total of £444.76 (£34.33, plus £62.65, plus £99.58, plus £57, plus £141, plus £50.20). In miniature this is a classic case, containing all those elements to which critics of the court-martial system have objected. In the case of the sergeant major they are as follows:

1. The prosecution (in effect the Army), given the choice of a District or a General Court Martial, has chosen the GCM, because it wants to inflict the maximum punishment on the sergeant major.

2. If found guilty, the sergeant major may face a punishment out of all proportion to his offence. He is likely to be thrown out of the Army and lose £60,000 gratuities, on which he was depending for his new life when he left the service. He is likely to go to prison, which would mean his wife and family might well lose their married quarters. If this was a civilian case brought to trial in a magistrate's court, the punishment for a theft of £444.76 can only be imagined, but it would certainly be minuscule by comparison.

3. A member of the armed forces has no automatic right to trial by civilian court.

4. The jury are all officers. There is no equivalent of the civilian jury, which should represent a cross-section of society. In the case of a GCM, which the sergeant major faces, the presiding officers must be of a certain rank, and, therefore, one supposes, of a certain type and ethos, imbued with Army thinking and Army codes of practice. The president must be a brigadier or colonel, and the four remaining officers that comprise the board (in effect the jury) must be of the rank of captain and above.

There is no escape from European legislation. Once more, as was the case with servicewomen compelled to leave the Army through pregnancy, and similarly with regard to homosexuals, an appeal is being made over the head of the British Parliament to Europe. The Human Rights Commission in Strasbourg is due to hear twelve test cases brought by Mr Gilbert Blades, a Lincoln solicitor with twenty years' experience defending servicemen in courts martial. The lead case is brought by an RAF sergeant who was given nine months' imprisonment and dismissed the service for 'threatening, abusive and insulting behaviour'. Other offences to be brought before the scrutiny of the European Court include assault, indecent assault, theft, undue familiarity with female subordinates, and (ominously) expenses fraud.

Britain is virtually alone in Europe in having a military system of justice running separately and in parallel with civilian procedures. Most European countries try their servicemen under military law in civilian courts. The court-martial system in Britain grew up because there needed to be a means of dispensing justice when ships or armies were away on campaign, particularly as expeditionary forces might find themselves in parts of the globe where concepts of justice were very different from those in Britain. There are also certain offences that are peculiar to the services, all devolving around the need to maintain discipline. A civilian is not compelled to go to work; he can tell his boss to get lost, he can go on indefinite strike. If a soldier does the first he is charged with being 'absent without leave' (AWOL), the second – disobedience, the third – mutiny. All three offences can result in stiff gaol terms. If there is one dead cert in the future, it is that the services and the European Convention on Human Rights are going to fall out seriously.

But this was of no consequence to the sergeant major who appeared at Catterick Court Martial Centre on 6 February, ten months after his arrest. At seven minutes past two, the Court Orderly, a Scottish sergeant in the Royal Logistical Corps, who was doing court-martial duty for the first time, bellowed, 'the Court is open'. There was a pause, then 'Apologies, the Court is not open', which was an omen, as it happened, for what was to follow.

The President of the Court and the four members of his panel, who had looked so ordinary on their way to court walking across the car park in lived-in corduroys and tweed jackets, carrying bags from the dry cleaners, now appeared in all their finery: service dress, No.1 dress cap, Sam Browne and cross-belt, sword and medals. They clanked across the Court and sat impressively and impassively in front of a Union Jack spread out on the wall behind.

There followed the prosecution, Capt. Susan Ridge, the Portia of Eastern Command, and the defence in the person of Jeremy Moon, of the civilian firm, Christopher Wright and Cohave. Jeremy Moon had had a distinguished military career. He had left the army as lieutenant colonel in the Army Legal Service. It was going to be fascinating watching the duel between this experienced operator and the intelligent Susan Ridge. Unfortunately, Susan Ridge was able to utter only one word before she was told to sit down by the Judge Advocate.

Jeremy Moon had objected to three of the five members of the jury panel, of whom, significantly, one was the president himself, Col. Leighton of the Adjutant General's Corps. The other two were Capt. Marsh, also of the AGC, and Maj. Earl of the Royal Regiment of Fusiliers. The Court Administrative Officer, Maj. (retired) Bill McGinty, whose job it is to organize the panel of officers, had quite sensibly, this being a technically difficult financial case, packed it with accountants and solicitors, men familiar with military fiscal practices.

'Not fair,' intoned Mr Moon. 'Specialist knowledge may be prejudicial to my client.' One can see the point he was trying to make. These senior Army officers, committed to the Army, with all their knowledge and expertise, would instinctively recoil from an expenses fraud, and they would be more inclined to find against rather than for the sergeant major. What Moon wanted was not financial experts, but ordinary, down-to-earth officers who would decide on much simpler criteria whether Purcell was dishonest or not. In other words, the sort of juryman ideally to be found in a Crown Court.

One felt for the sergeant major. He had endured six months of hell, gearing himself up for this ordeal. But no sooner was he marched in, hatless and beltless, to face his accusers, than he was marched out again.

It took another four months for the trial to reconvene. This time Jeremy Moon was satisfied with Maj. McGinty's choice of officers. There was not an accountant among them; these were five good officers and true.

Before the sergeant major's trial began, there was another court martial in which Jeremy Moon unsuccessfully defended a certain WO2 Purvis, who was convicted of stealing DM7,000 from a Deutsches Telecom coin-operated

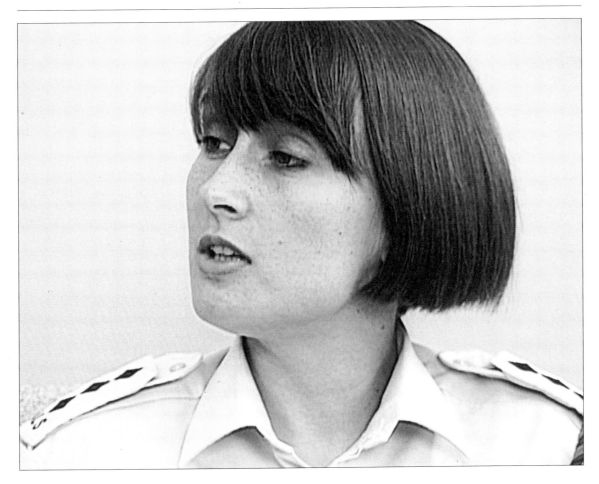

telephone in Osnabrück to feed his obsession with fruit machines. Although Purvis pleaded guilty, and had a psychiatrist as expert witness to testify to his disorder, he was sentenced to six months' imprisonment, dismissed from the service and reduced to the ranks. That sentence cost him his gratuity on completion of twenty-two years' service and his service pension – a round figure of £100,000. Purvis was clearly shaken at the severity of the sentence, and so were those in the courtroom.

Capt. (now Major) Susan Ridge – a rising star in the Army's Legal Service.

No one failed to notice that Purcell was of the same rank as Purvis, would be defended by the same man, Jeremy Moon, and would soon face the same jury. As if the savage sentence handed out to Purvis still hung in the air, both defence and the Judge Advocate himself mistakenly called Purcell 'Purvis' on a number of occasions in the trial that followed.

But before that trial could start, there was a delay of four hours. Almost immediately after the conclusion of the Purvis trial, Jeremy Moon had unexpectedly offered a deal to the prosecution in the case of Purcell. His client would plead guilty to the three charges – Charge 2, 5 and 6, involving sums of £62.65, £141, and £50.20 – provided that charges 1, 3 and 4 were dropped.

This changed things dramatically. The sergeant major was now admitting to the submission of phoney receipts on three occasions. He had simply got into a muddle. He knew he had to account for the cash advances, but as he had also lost the originals, he had submitted false receipts. The alternative would have been repaying the cash advances from his own pocket.

Maj. Ridge readily accepted the plea bargain. Whether the sergeant major was guilty of three charges or six was not the nub of the matter. It was a question of integrity. She accepted that in submitting the phoney receipts the sergeant major had not profited personally.

It remained now to decide on the sentence. Reports were read. They were glowing, and years of unblemished service were cited. The Adjutant reported that the sergeant major had left school at the age of fifteen without 'O' levels, but had worked hard and improved himself in the Army. He was a committed family man with three children. As he was due soon to leave the Army when he reached forty, he was buying a house in Scotland.

Then Jeremy Moon rose. 'You have heard from Capt. McIntosh [the Adjutant] that the sergeant major is not a person equipped with a high degree of literacy or numeracy. He has had to struggle to keep up to date in his job. When he joined the Army in 1971 there were no computers or computerized systems. Nevertheless, a man whose whole life had been as a cook was, when appointed Regimental Messing Officer, suddenly expected to be an accountant. Mr Purcell has received no training in these accounts, or in a system that was complicated. He simply got into a muddle. He tried to get out of it as best he could. . . Mr Purcell is in almost every respect a down-to-earth, old-time soldier. In a sticky situation he is the sort of chap you would want by your side.

'He has only a very, very short time to serve. On completion of that service he will receive a terminal grant and annual pension. [Much of this would be forfeit if the sergeant major received the same sentence as WO2 Purvis.] He is very remorseful that he tried to fudge things when he got into a mess. I ask the Court to bear in mind that, by pleading guilty, my client will have a criminal record on the national computer, which will make job-finding difficult.'

The sergeant major publicly regretted what he had done and apologized to the Court. The Court then rose. After lunch, the President announced the sentence – a fine of £500 and a reprimand. That was that. The sergeant major heaved a huge sigh of relief. His life, that could so easily have been ruined, was still intact.

It had taken fourteen months and innumerable man hours to bring this matter to a conclusion. The Redcaps had investigated meticulously. They had interviewed the sergeant major twice and taken statements from scores of witnesses among authorized dealers in York itself as well as in the kitchens and offices of Imphal Barracks. Keen legal minds had wrestled with the difficulties and ambiguities of the case. Two courts martial had been convened. So was it worth all the time and effort?

Lt Col Dick Austin of Army Legal had this to say: 'The Army is primarily interested in this kind of case with integrity. If you're just talking cost, you may well say this hasn't been cost effective. But if you're saying that, you say integrity is worth nothing. That is not a proposition with which I happen to agree.'

In a way, the verdict was the last thing that mattered, except to the sergeant major. It had been an illuminating episode casting light on that interface between the Redcaps and the Army Legal Service, and the Army Legal Service and the increasingly controversial court-martial system.

CHAPTER 7

THE WIFE, THE CORPORAL, THE OFFICER AND THEIR LOVERS

'F—! The f—ing f—er's f—ed!' I once heard this example of the notorious F-word used as interjection, adjective, noun and verb to describe a rifle whose bolt mechanism was jammed. (The 'I' in this case is 23068908 Pte Mills R. of the Royal Army Service Corps, National Service 1954–56 and co-author of this book.) It is no surprise that this Anglo-Saxon four-letter-word that means 'to have sexual intercourse with' should be the most used word in the British Army.

Although the Army is an Equal Opportunities Employer, it is predominantly male: of the 123,028 servicepersons in the Army, only 7,052 are female. Most of the 115,976 males are in the eighteen to thirty age range, a time of life when the thoughts and activities of the young soldier are often directed towards sex, real or imaginary. What ex-soldier will ever forget the rude awakening at reveille by his corporal: 'Hands off cocks, and on with your socks!'? What National-Serviceman can erase from his memory the 1950s equivalent of the condom vending machine – the furtive stranger who frequented the barrack-blocks with his hoarse offer, 'Any of you boys need a French letter?'

But things have changed. The reading matter of the average squaddie is the Sun and the Sport. He has seen and fantasized over the girls in the soft-porn magazines. They adorn the walls above his bed-space – a vision of heaven in a drab barrack-block. He has visited the auto-erotic video-cabins of the Reeperbahn in Hamburg and Oudezijds Voorburgwal in Amsterdam. In everything that he sees and reads, he is told that girls 'want it', 'hot and strong', and 'often'. An unmarried soldier's life, when he is not on duty or exercise, is drinking, fighting and bonking. And when the girls, the objects of his desire, do not react to his clumsy overtures in the textbook manner of the *Sun*, or *Men Only*, then there is trouble, and the RMP become involved.

The Army would rather all its soldiers behaved in a decent civilized way, but it knows that is asking too much. The lewd, licentious soldiery have always raped, looted and pillaged. Indeed, rape, loot and pillage were often seen as a justifiable perk after the privations of a long hard campaign – provided things did not get out of hand. In modern times, when the nature of war has changed, the Army has adopted a philosophy of damage limitation – free condoms at the medical centre, lectures and films on AIDS, and the pursuit of alleged sexual offenders through the RMP.

The case for the young soldier has been eloquently argued by the CO of the Royal Green Jackets, who wrote to a woman who had been punched, called 'a slag' and soaked in drink in an unprovoked attack by some drunken soldiers from his regiment in the sunshine posting of Cyprus. The CO said, 'I command nearly 650 men (with an average age of twenty-two), and much as I would wish them to be paragons of virtue, they cannot be expected to survive two and a half years in Cyprus without causing trouble.'

The other big change is in the squaddie's social status. As a youngster of eighteen with not much education, he has a secure job, with the likelihood of adventure, prospects for travel, and a disposable income of about £600 a month. In these days he is quite a catch, and in the garrison towns of Britain and Germany, there are girls who see in him the answer to all their problems. For their prospects of owning a home are dim. The only marriage they see is the unmarried motherhood which leads to cohabitation with the DSS and a leap-frog up the local council housing-list.

Strictly speaking, it is against regulations for girls to stay overnight in Army barracks. But this is a somewhat grey area. If a soldier meets his girlfriend at the guardroom and escorts her to one of the on-camp bars, or discos, or social events, and she stays the night, what offence has been committed? A soldier is over eighteen. His billet is his home, and he has rights, the same as anyone else. And if a girl sneaks in to see Private X when Private Y is on gate duty, why, at another time another girl may sneak in to see Private Y when Private X is on gate duty.

In the discos of Celle and Osnabrück, Colchester and Aldershot, the girls dress to kill. A good night out can lead to a bunk-up in the barracks, a pregnancy, a teenage marriage, a child, then another, and a home. As the 'Wives' Guide to the Army' says, 'When you married a soldier, you became part of the Army Family'. Above all, this means that the Army supplies a soldier with furnished married quarters.

Such marriages are extremely vulnerable. A new wife has to learn quickly that, technically, her new husband is

In 1989 the MoD was forced to give financial compensation to women who had been dismissed from the Army on the grounds that they had become pregnant.

JOIN THE ARMY AND SEE THE CHEQUE!

"I never thought when I joined the Army that I'd end up a millionaire! But, thanks to EC discrimination rules, my pregnancy earned me £300,000. Not bad, eh, for a night exercise!"

ARMY RATES IN FULL

Loss of limb in battle	0p
Loss of life in Ulster	3p
Loss of life in WWII	1 poppy
Bun in oven	300 grand

JUST LIE BACK AND THINK OF THE BANK OF ENGLAND!

The death-threat letter to soldier's wife Kerry Martinson.

on duty twenty-four hours a day, seven days a week, that he can be posted away from her to places such as Northern Ireland and Bosnia, where she will not be allowed to accompany him. Alone, with a young family in bleak married quarters, far removed from her own parents and friends, she is prey to boredom and loneliness. Around her there are hordes of agencies dying to be helpful – the Federation of Army Wives, Home Start, Families Housing and Welfare service, HIVES (Help, Information, Volunteer Exchange), and not least, the Colonel's wife. But a young Army wife can fall quickly into adultery, when her husband is away, with dire consequences on his return (for there are few secrets on an Army base). However chaste she is, she can all too easily become the victim of obscene phone calls and threatening letters. At this point the RMP can become involved.

One graphic example. On 5 July 1994, an attractive young mother wheeled a pram into Imphal Barracks, York, with two little boys in tow. She stopped outside the block that housed the SIB of the RMP. She was an army wife, her name was Kerry, and her children were Jonathan aged 5, David aged 3 and Ashlea aged 3 1/2 months.

Kerry was terrified. She had received a death-threat in the post scrawled in crude capital letters. The letter said, 'YOU AND YOUR FUCKING BOYFRIEND ARE DEAD. SWEET DREAMS, BABE.' As a result, there was no question of sleep, let alone dreams. The case was now in the hands of Sgt Billy Walkins, RMP, and the prime suspect was Kerry's estranged husband, Nick. Theirs had been a tempestuous relationship. In Walkins' office was a canvas of an Alpine scene, that had once adorned Kerry's sitting-room wall. It had been a wedding present. On the back was written, 'Kerry, no matter what happens, I love you and the boys, despite what you think. So please reconsider what you're doing.' This had been written by Nick after Kerry could endure no more, and had walked out. While the rest of the detectives (or investigators as they are called in the SIB) set about the unaccustomed task of distracting two lively toddlers, Sgt Walkins began to elicit from Kerry a sad and sordid story of sexual jealousy, drunkenness and violence in the married quarters of Catterick and Osnabrück.

Kerry was already pregnant by another man when she and Nick were married in 1989. The violence started four weeks into the marriage. He would kick her and throw things at her despite the pregnancy. As she was a newly-wed, she said nothing, but the attacks continued. Eventually, the unit was posted to Germany.

Things got worse as the rumour mills churned out allegations that Kerry was having affairs, or Kerry 'fancied' other men, or Kerry was being flirtatious. One evening, said Kerry, 'Nick just flipped. He came over to the bed and put his hands around my neck, and just kept, like, trying to strangle me. I was lying on the bed, slowly losing my breath, and it got to the stage where I thought, "I'm not going to get the better of him here", so I just lay there and I thought I wasn't going to take another breath.'

But Kerry did not die. Nick suddenly seemed to pull himself together. He jumped off the bed and ran out of the door. 'I sat and cried,' said Kerry. 'Then, after half an hour or so, I decided that I'd pretend it never happened. I'd go down to camp, meet him at camp, give him a kiss as if it never happened. Because I pretended nothing had happened, so did he.'

Kerry later spoke to the Families Officer and Nick was removed from his married quarters, and told to take up single quarters in the camp. But by this time Nick had heard that his wife was having an affair with her baby-sitter, Matthew Martinson, who was also in Nick's unit, the Prince of Wales Own. Martinson was one of Nick's friends. He had introduced him to his wife.

One hot early evening, Nick entered the married quarters through the open balcony door. He stood in the bedroom shaking and crying. 'I knew I was going to get hit,' said Kerry, 'so I thought it would be better to get him outside. That way people wouldn't think I was shouting at my kids. He asked me to get into the car with him, and I refused because of other occasions when he'd driven like a madman, if things were tense between us. The next thing I knew, he'd pushed me against a pebble-dash wall, sunk his teeth into my cheek, and had his hands around my neck. Once he'd let go of his teeth from my cheek, he pulled back his fist to hit me, and, it's a bit hazy that bit, I just remember seeing the fist coming back.

'The next thing I knew, I was lying on the floor with a nose bleed, and then he started kicking me repeatedly in the head. All of a sudden he started running away, and I did wonder why. I hadn't realized that a RMP who lived above me had seen the attack from his kitchen window.'

Sgt Walkins asked Kerry why she thought Nick had sunk his teeth into her cheek. She said, 'He was going to take a chunk out of my cheek, so that I'd be scarred.'

Martinson was also attacked. He was in bed when the door burst open. Two men rushed in. Nick and a private from the same regiment. One of them carried a hammer. Martinson was hit on the head and the back. He pleaded with his assailants not to touch his knees as he was suffering from a skiing accident incurred on an Army exercise. Martinson went on, 'But they did my knees and then rammed the hammer in my mouth. I lost two lots of teeth. He was threatening me that if I went to see Kerry, I'd be dead. This was only a slight thing. Next time I'd come off a lot worse.'

After the assault, Martinson staggered bleeding to the Medical Centre and said that he had fallen down the stairs. But it was obvious to everyone that he was lying. By now Martinson wanted out. He wanted to be discharged from the Army, so that he could be with Kerry. The matter eventually reached the CO, and according to Martinson, the regimental solution was a plea-bargain, of which the RMP strongly disapproved.

The Regiment told Martinson that he was entitled to give evidence against Nick in a court martial, but this would take a long time to convene, and so delay his discharge. There was no certainty that there would be a conviction. Alternatively, an easier solution would be if he agreed to accept the charge of 'Fighting', for which he would get twenty-eight days' detention. He would then be given his discharge, and the whole matter could be contained within the regiment.

Martinson accepted regimental advice and took the easier option. He pleaded guilty to something he said he had not done. Sgt Walkins was later to visit the regiment in Germany to fire a warning shot across the bows for putting pressure on a soldier to waive his rights.

Kerry Martinson (she has taken Matthew's name) is terrified to be left alone in the house in York. Since the assault, Martinson can no longer sleep on a bed. The death-threat letter disturbs their peace of mind.

The sexual activities of the officer class are more discreet. On the whole, officers do not frequent discos or raves and their courtship rituals owe less to the caveman. But that does not mean that officers are gentlemen. Occasionally the firmament is briefly lit up by some garish display of officerly passion; a 'Captain Crumpet' or a 'Bonking Brigadier' arrives to enliven the breakfast table.

Occasionally a chink of light shows between the curtains of the officers' mess of an elite regiment, through which a peeping Tom may sometimes observe toga parties – quasi-sexual rituals of subalterns at play, when their elders and betters are tucked up in bed with their wives. As a second lieutenant in the very upper-crust Royal Horse Artillery, Alistair Green was called 'ten-inch' because his penis was thought to be rather tiny. He claimed that he was repeatedly stripped naked by his brother officers, and was once strapped naked to a cannon with a rose between his buttocks.

In its handling of sexual peccadilloes, the Army very definitely lines up on the side of Virtue. It is against adultery, against fornication, and against homosexuality. It is against the abuse of rank to gain sexual favours and it is against officers having affairs with other ranks. It is against officers and other ranks marrying. The Army would prefer breeding to occur in an orderly and disciplined way, officer with officer, sergeant with sergeant, holders of the Queen's Commission with holders of the Queen's Commission.

To some extent the RMP sees itself as an upholder of the Army's moral code, and Lt. Col. Nelson, who is currently the head of RMP in Southern

Time Euro Disco, Bergen, Germany – where soldier meets soldier meets fraulein meets trouble.

Command, occasionally gets out from his Aldershot base to lecture officers and men on the Army's stern morality code – a task rendered almost impossible when the Chief of the Defence Staff fell very publicly into the bed of a young lady, who promptly told the press all about it.

In most adult institutions, adultery is held to be a personal matter, and authority is loath to get involved, but not in the Army, where it is regarded as 'a serious form of misconduct'. If a CO or the Ministry of Defence receives a formal complaint from a husband or wife, it will be investigated through the Redcaps' plainclothes detectives, the SIB, who will submit a report on the incident to the Army Board. There are a range of sanctions, from a verbal rebuke from the officer's CO, to a demand for the officer to resign his commission.

There are currently forty officers awaiting discharge from the Army for 'Disgraceful Behaviour' – the Army's description for adultery. It is a sign of the times that these Breakers of the Seventh Commandment have shown a marked reluctance to do the decent thing and go quickly. They point out that the Heir to the Throne, who is Colonel-in-Chief of not a few regiments, has admitted on television an affair with the wife of the recently retired Director of the Royal Army Veterinary and Remount Services, and that if they are expected to fall meekly on their swords, then so should he. Their argument is likely to fall on stony ground. It will be pointed out that they are on the Active List, while the Prince of Wales is not. In matters of morality, that, apparently, makes all the difference.

It is in problems posed by seniority in rank that difficulties can arise. In the Army, junior ranks are conditioned to jump to an order, to obey it instantly and without question if ordered to by someone senior. While no real difficulty arises if that order is 'Quick march' or 'About turn', it is another matter if the order is 'Knickers down!' This is no hypothetical example of a fevered imagination. It happened.

We will have to call her Pte Brown. She is on a NATO exercise. She falls into a ditch and sprains a muscle on the outside of her leg. To alleviate the pain, she goes to the medical tent for some cream to rub on to the sore spot. But the medical warrant officer has other ideas. He asks her to take off her combat trousers and lie on the examination couch. Although the injury is to her outer leg, he squirts his cream on to Pte Brown's inner thigh. Sgt Maj. Karen Miller of the SIB conducted the enquiry that followed the misdeed.

SGT MILLER: How far up the leg did he go?

PTE BROWN: He was touching my pubic hair, manipulating the flesh

around there. And he said, 'Would you take your knickers off'. I guess I was just scared, and looking back, I know I shouldn't have done it, but I just did what he said. I trusted him and I just did it.

SGT MILLER: What underwear were you wearing?

PTE BROWN: Just a pair of knickers.

SGT MILLER: Brief type knickers?

PTE BROWN: Yeah. Just, you know, little ones . . . Not skimpy, just . . .

SGT MILLER: And what were your feelings when he actually asked you to remove your underwear?

PTE BROWN: Well, I guess I was shocked, but I felt I had to do it, as it's what he told me.

It is not always easy for a young, impressionable person to distinguish between a legal and an illegal order.

The disbanding of the Women's Royal Army Corps in 1992 no doubt made good sense to accountants. But its disappearance after forty-three years has turned some young women into rather forlorn figures. There was a pastoral fall-back in the WRAC, a shoulder to cry on, motherly and sisterly advice. Scattered now through the male units, female soldiers are still objects of lechery if they are pretty, and objects of scorn if they are not; but gone is the all-feminine bolt-hole, her comfort and escape. In order to survive she has to build around herself strong psychological barriers.

But the RMP took the attempted seduction of Pte Brown very seriously. It would have liked to put an end to the medical warrant officer's amorous practices, but there was no corroboration. It was her word against his, and in

Sgt Maj. Karen Miller, RMP, listens intently as 'Pte Brown' describes how she was sexually molested by a medical warrant officer.

the end the matter was dropped.

There is no ambiguity about the Army's stance on homosexuality. With the Royal Navy and Royal Air Force it stands like a rock in shifting sands, utterly and implacably opposed to all homos, woofters and weirdos. It does not – indeed, legally it cannot – prosecute them, since it must be in step with current legislation. But homosexuality is deemed incompatible with service in the Forces. As Julian Brazier of the Conservative backbench defence committee imaginatively pointed out, 'Servicemen very often share facilities together, sometimes as many as fifteen or twenty people in a dormitory. The idea of a pair of homosexuals making love at night with eighteen other people in the room would outrage people.' The thought of such nocturnal writhings certainly outrages the Army.

Homosexuals are booted out. Indeed, in the last four years 259 gay or lesbian servicepersons have suffered this indignity, including four majors, four captains, an RAF squadron leader and two chaplains. To avoid such unpleasantness in the first place, recruits are read the following statement at their first interview: 'Because it is incompatible with service in the armed forces, any kind of homosexual activity will constitute grounds for administrative discharge from the Army.' Recruits are asked if they understand the statement. While it may deter some, it appears not to discourage all.

The pursuit and 'outing' of recusant gays falls straight into the remit of the SIB. Word will reach them by anonymous letter, by telephone call, by direct complaint, by 'information received', or by their own investigative methods. (The SIB will always attempt to get a suspect to 'name names' or incriminate his friends, be it a question of drugs, theft, or homosexuality.)

The first thing that will happen to a new suspect is the swoop search. Two SIB investigators will unexpectedly arrive and comb his or her accommodation. Diaries, letters, videos, photographs, may be taken away. There follows an in-depth taped interview aimed at establishing the truth or not of the allegation. But that in itself is not enough. To ensure that the subject is not using the excuse of homosexuality to get out of the Army cheaply (normally a soldier would have to buy himself out, if he wants to leave the Army before he has completed his contractual term), homosexuality has to be proved. The suspect must give detailed descriptions of how and (conveniently) with whom he has had sex. Gay men may have their anal sphincters examined to establish if intercourse has taken place. The names of homosexuals and suspected homosexuals, male and female, are stored in the Royal Military Police's computer at their Central Criminal Records and Intelligence Office (CCRIO).

SSgt Dale Pitt of CCRIO revealed that the latest yearly figures for 'male on male' sexual offences was 243. These were not necessarily homosexual offences, we were assured. Dale Pitt gave us an insight from his records into what the Redcaps define as a male-on-male sexual (but not homosexual) offence.

'It was in Germany in 1993. It was, like, an initiation ceremony. The guys were all drunk, and one of them made him [the initiate] suck his dick. In another, a guy had a roll of paper stuck up his arse and set it alight. These are not homosexual cases, but they are sexually-orientated assaults.' This boys-will-be-boys attitude, however, ceases the moment that the torment becomes something sensual. Two RMP officers were discussing that interesting moment when sexual turns homosexual.

'If we caught one para sucking off another, we wouldn't call that gay.' The other agreed, 'He was just doing it to shock. That's what soldiers are like.'

'But if the para who was sucked off said, "I like that, can we do it again tomorrow?" that's gay, and he's out.'

This cosy world in which the Army can be sexually cleansed by the Redcaps is in danger. An army of 'homophiles' is flexing its muscles against the homophobes. The Labour Party says that, if elected, it would allow homosexuals to enlist. The Army would certainly resist, just as the American military establishment locked horns with President Clinton, when he attempted to legislate gays into the US forces. But there is an even greater danger – European legislation, to which this country is a signatory, and on which the Ministry of Defence has so far shown a somewhat shaky grasp. An unhappy precedent for the Ministry was its sacking of pregnant servicewomen in the 1970s and 1980s, which is against the European sex discrimination law. The blunder has so far cost the British taxpayer over £30 million in compensation, a legal bill on which no one will place a figure, and there are a further 1,494 cases outstanding.

The omens for Ministry of Defence policy towards homosexuals do not look promising. A shudder ran through the Ministry in March 1995. A High Court judge allowed former senior aircraftwoman, Jeanette Smith, leave to bring a High Court case against the Ministry of Defence for dismissing her because she was a lesbian. Significantly, permission was granted under the same European anti-sex discrimination laws used by the pregnant servicewomen. The test case, which is legally-aided by the homosexual pressure group Stonewall, is being heard in the European Court of Justice in Luxemburg in 1995. If it is successful, the floodgates will open as surely as they opened when the pregnant servicewomen won their case. Some 300 homosexual ex-servicepersons are waiting to demand compensation. More serious from a homophobic Army point of view is that the military's antagonistic policy towards homosexuals would be blown out of the water, and, whether it wanted to or not, it would have to join Belgium, France, Israel, Spain and the Netherlands in giving employment to gay soldiers.

To their avowed relief, most of the sex crimes the Redcaps deal with are heterosexual. In 1994, they dealt with a total of 183 rapes, attempted rapes and indecent assaults. We were given a unique insight into an SIB rape investigation, when the accused allowed us to record his interrogation by the SIB. One condition was that his identity was to be preserved, so he will be referred to as Cpl A. The assault victims, who gave statements and appeared as witnesses must be legally protected, and they too will be referred to by letter.

In the early hours of Friday 24 June, two corporals entered the female sleeping accommodation of a barracks in Leicestershire. Later, five women soldiers alleged that Cpl A touched them indecently. The SIB was brought in. Sgt Chappell spent a week investigating the case and persuading the girls to give statements. Some were reluctant, but Sgt Chappell is a rising star. He is persuasive and friendly. He obtained his evidence, and shot a video of the accommodation so that the layout would be understood. Then Cpl A was summoned for interview.

Cpl A is black. Facing him was the young Sgt Chappell and the large bulk of the experienced SIB Warrant Officer Class 2, Kevin Morson. Morson said nothing, leaving the interview to his young colleague, but his presence was palpable. To Cpl A's right was a tape recorder; behind him a camera crew. The interview was conducted strictly in accordance with the Police and Criminal Evidence Act (PACE). There was no hectoring, no bullying, but Cpl A was led into traps from which it was impossible to escape.

After the legal formalities, Sgt Chappell began to spring his traps. Did Cpl A have a nickname? Cpl A told him what it was. Did he smoke? Yes, he did. Had he had a sexual relationship with any of the complainants? He hadn't. Had he touched any of the girls in the camp indecently? He hadn't. What happened on the night in question? Cpl A said that he had been celebrating his friend's completion of twenty-two years' service in the British Army, plus his own last day in uniform. After fourteen years in the Army, he was leaving to take up a place at Bristol University. They returned to camp at 1.30 in the morning. Cpl A felt a little 'tipsy'. A girl shouted 'Hey, there's a party in here. Come on.' Cpl A's companion, LCpl H (name also withheld) entered the block but Cpl A returned to his own room.

SGT CHAPPELL: So at no point did you ever go into the female accommodation?

CPL A: No, I tried to persuade Cpl H not to go in because it was 'out of bounds'.

SGT CHAPPELL: The reason I asked you to come to interview today is because it is alleged that you indecently assaulted some of the females in the camp that night. Could you give me any explanation why somebody would make these allegations against you?

Cpl A explains that he is the RP Corporal, the Regimental Provost Corporal, in charge of discipline in the camp, making the soldiers march correctly, and seeing to it that they are properly turned out. As such he is not much liked, as he is zealous, authoritarian and a killjoy. In his opinion, the women soldiers have ganged up to have their revenge on him on his last day in uniform.

Sgt Chappell strikes:

SGT CHAPPELL: About five girls have come forward independently and told us that night you touched them indecently in the early hours of Friday.

CPL A: No, I did not do that.

SGT CHAPPELL: Another girl, Pte B, told us on Saturday 30 April this year you came into her room where she was sleeping in her bed and laid on top of her. You had an erect penis and you were forcing it against her knickers towards her vagina.

CPL A: No. I didn't do none of that.

SGT CHAPPELL: These five girls all came forward independently. And there are other girls who witnessed your name being called out in expressions like 'fuck off . . . [Chappell uses the nickname he has already elicited from Cpl A].

CPL A: Yes . . .

SGT CHAPPELL: 'or go away . . .' A number of those girls saw you leaving those rooms in the early hours of that morning. Or heard your distinctive voice as they've described it to me.

CPL A: Er huh.

SGT CHAPPELL: And the girls themselves, all the girls who've come forward, have all said they recognized it was you.

CPL A: I can only say that it's untrue. I did not go in the block at all.

SGT CHAPPELL: So why would all these people then come forward?

CPL A: I don't know.

SGT CHAPPELL: Well, Cpl A, all these people have come forward voluntarily.

CPL A: I did not go past the steps on that night. I only stopped LCpl H going in any further.

SGT CHAPPELL: OK then, if that's your explanation of it. What were you smoking that night? [Sgt Chappell has closed off any exit that Cpl A is a non-smoker, earlier in the preamble to the interview.]

CPL A: I don't - erm, I normally smoke erm, Super King Blues.

SGT CHAPPELL: And what were you using as something to light it? What were you using?

CPL A: Just a lighter.

[Sgt Chappell reaches under the desk and produces a lighter, which he shows to Cpl A.]

No, that's not mine. That is not mine.

SGT CHAPPELL: One of the girls, a lance corporal, came forward and described what happened to her. She made no allegation of assault against herself. She claimed she threw you out of her room. She said once she got in to bed, where you'd been sat, she lent against that [indicating the lighter] after you'd gone.

CPL A: Er huh.

SGT CHAPPELL: And she says no one else was in her room that night.

CPL A: That's not my lighter.

SGT CHAPPELL: Are you sure about that?

CPL A: I'm positive.

SGT CHAPPELL: Well, she's positive it's yours.

Then Sgt Chappell sprang his cleverest trap.

SGT CHAPPELL: Let's turn to Pte B then. How well do you know Pte B?

CPL A: From the guardroom I know all the girls personally 'cos when they come into the unit they come into the guardroom and they spend a short spell there working and doing odd jobs and they're around – so you get to speak to them.

SGT CHAPPELL: OK. Do you like her?

CPL A: What as, as a friend?

SGT CHAPPELL: As anything.

CPL A: She's OK. Nothing special.

SGT CHAPPELL: Ever fancied her?

CPL A: No.

SGT CHAPPELL: Are you sure?

CPL A: Yes.

SGT CHAPPELL: Ever had sexual intercourse with her?

CPL A: No.

SGT CHAPPELL: Never attacked her in her bed?

CPL A: No, definitely not.

SGT CHAPPELL: Why does she claim that you did?

CPL A: I don't know.

SGT CHAPPELL: Why, when we questioned her later about other evidence we found out, did she very, very embarrassedly admit that she had had sexual intercourse with you once before the attack?

CPL A: No, I've never had any sexual intercourse with her.

SGT CHAPPELL: Are you sure?

CPL A: Yes.

SGT CHAPPELL: She also keeps a diary. [A very long pause. Sgt Chappell holds eye contact with Cpl A. Suddenly Chappell reaches again under the desk] and in the diary she gave to us, I'll read it out to you. 'I went to Crystals Night Club. Got off with a Welsh lad. He's really nice but there's Colin – Colin's her boyfriend, she admits that. 'Anyway, he had to leave earlier because of guard duty, so I got off with a black corporal RP. We had sex in his penthouse. I didn't get in till 5 am, so I only had an hour's kip.' That's on the Friday 22 April.

CPL A: No. Again, no.

WO1 MORSON: Why did she write that then?

CPL A: I don't know.

SGT CHAPPELL: Cpl A, who else is black and in the RP in that unit?

CPL A: I'm the only black person there.

SGT CHAPPELL: OK. So why then, later, did she write this in her personal diary. [He reads] [Pte B names Cpl A] . . . came to my room – woke me up at 3.15 am. The twat, he really fancies me – he stripped and wanted to have sex. As if . . .'

There is another long pause as the cat and mouse continues.

CPL A: Don't know. I don't know where all this is coming from. I've never been with any of the women there and I've never been in that accommodation.

Cpl H admitted going into the women's quarters. He signed a statement saying that Cpl A went there as well. He also said that Cpl A made strenuous efforts next day to see him. Sgt Chappell assumed that Cpl A, knowing the seriousness of what happened, was trying to get an agreed version of events with H to the effect that neither of them went into the rooms.

SGT CHAPPELL: I think you knew what was happening, why you wanted to speak to him desperately.

CPL A: I didn't want to speak to him desperately.

SGT CHAPPELL: Cpl K then came forward to me.

CPL A: Yeah.

SGT CHAPPELL: You know, a very senior junior NCO.

CPL A: Yeah.

SGT CHAPPELL: And what he said you said to him was – this is your words to him: 'All I did was what any other drunken squaddie would want to do. Touch up girls when they're asleep.'

CPL A: I don't think so.

SGT CHAPPELL: OK. What Cpl K also says is you went up to the male accommodation, where he followed you into your room which is at the top of the stairs virtually, isn't it?

CPL A: Yeah.

SGT CHAPPELL: You then walked in. Never put your light on – went straight in. Took some condoms and walked out and he then saw you from your window walking back towards the female accommodation.

CPL A: I didn't go back.

One by one Sgt Chappell hammered home the names of all the girls who claimed to have seen him that night.

SGT CHAPPELL: I personally can't believe that all these people have come forward and told me this and they're all lying.

CPL A: All I can say is that I didn't do it and I can see the evidence mounting up against me and if I had done it I would say. But I did not do these things.

SGT CHAPPELL: OK. Pte C recalls you coming into the room. And you asked for a goodnight kiss.

CPL A: No. I didn't kiss her.

SGT CHAPPELL: She then says that you came back to her room later on when she was asleep, later on that morning – two o'clock, say.

CPL A: Yeah.

SGT CHAPPELL: And she threw you out of her room. That's when she found the lighter.

CPL A: Er huh.

SGT CHAPPELL: OK, she then heard Pte D. Pte D tells me she was in bed naked and watching TV and she was sort of dozing. She covered herself up and you started asking her a number of things. Then you put your hands over her duvet so she couldn't really move and you tried to kiss her face but she wouldn't let you and then you started to nip her.

OK, let's turn to Pte E. She claimed you came in to her room. You then later returned and touched her breasts. Pte F who lives in the same room just a partition away says she heard you say 'I know you want it'. She then saw it was you leaving the bed space of Pte E.

CPL A: I didn't. No, definitely not.

SGT CHAPPELL: And then there's Pte B, the young seventeen-year-old lass who says that it was 29 April and you came into her room – laid on top of her.

CPL A: No.

SGT CHAPPELL: So ten people outside here today are all wrong and you're right.

CPL A: I just know what is the truth and I did not do what's alleged (sic) against me.

The interview lasted one hour, and the transcript above is a heavily condensed version of an ordeal by inquisition. But Cpl A never wavered. He protested his innocence throughout. Perhaps unwisely. Had he, like Cpl H, admitted that he was drunk that evening, had gone into the female quarters, but only talked to the girls, things might have been different. As it was, at 3.25 Sgt Chappell concluded the interview with these words: 'There is sufficient evidence to justify disciplinary action being taken against you for attempted rape and indecent assault under the service disciplinary acts. A report will be submitted without delay to your commanding officer and other service authorities. You do not have to say anything unless you wish to do so, what

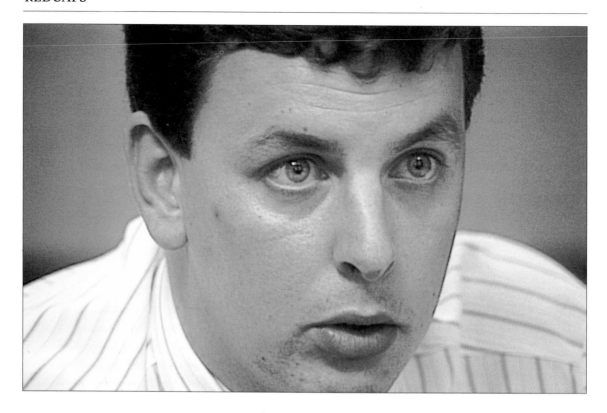

Sgt Mark Chappell, SIB – a master of eye contact and the use of silence.

you say may be given in evidence. The time is now 15.26 hours and this interview is now concluded.'

Cpl A spoke to us after the interview. He was sweating profusely and was angry: 'I'm a hated person there. I make their life misery and all the rest of it. I don't know why they said this. I don't even know where it's sprung up from. Four of the girls that have been mentioned there, they're – sorry to use the wrong words for it – but they're the biggest sluts. They jump into people's beds while the guy is out, and they come back just to get the guy. I myself know the rules better than anybody else. I've got more to lose than anybody else. I'm going to university, I'm buying my house, I'm getting my redundancy. I've completed fourteen years, yeah. I've bought my house, I've got my girlfriend. Yeah. We're planning to live together, and today, I hear all these allegations. Anybody in their right mind wouldn't go and do something stupid like that with the risk of getting into trouble. That's a person who is insane. You just don't do things like that.'

But if matters came to a court martial, Cpl A's case was going to be very difficult to prove against the weight of evidence. If he lost, the chances were that he would lose his stripes and serve a custodial sentence. Even worse than that: in jeopardy was his redundancy, the basis on which he intended to build his new life as a graduate in civvy street. After fourteen blameless years in the British Army, this amounted to £45,000.

CHAPTER 8

CRIME AND PUNISHMENT

When the Redcaps were done with Cpl A there was still plenty of work to be done. The file on the case was now a book, and that book, containing all the evidence gleaned by Sgt Chappell, was copied and sent off to Commander Legal, who would frame the charges. It also went to Cpl A's CO. This was no mere courtesy. A CO alone decides whether a case shall go forward to court martial. If he thinks it should not, he can dismiss it, or hear it himself. In effect the CO has the powers of a magistrate. He can sentence a soldier to up to twenty-eight days' detention, and up to twenty-eight days' loss of pay. If his brigadier allows him 'extended powers' he can double both punishments. But a CO would be very foolhardy to go it alone and ignore the advice of the Army Legal Service. Few do.

Late in July, Lt. Col. Dick Austin, Army Legal Eastern Command in York, spoke on the phone to Cpl A's CO. In front of him was the Redcaps' dossier of evidence.

'I'm just trying to get the case together . . . what I'm hoping to do is take it

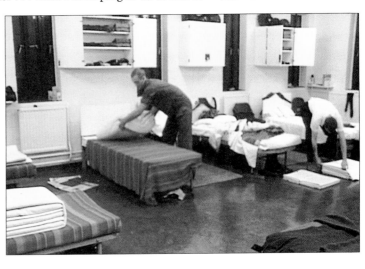

Reveille in a barrack room in the 'Glasshouse', Colchester.

away with me over the weekend and give you fairly detailed advice . . . Obviously, you must make up your own mind. It's your decision, and if you want to disagree with it, that doesn't worry me in the slightest. I've got plenty of other cases to get on with . . .

'I'm a little concerned about the first one, the seventeen-year-old [Pte B]. She in effect has not told the truth in her first statement [Pte B had made two statements to the SIB which did not tally in some important respects] and then she was found out when the SIB very properly

C Wing in the Glasshouse, where serious offenders, including murderers, are locked up.

did an investigation . . . That obviously makes her a very weak witness . . . She's going to have a torrid time if we try to bring that charge [of attempted rape], and having had a torrid time, we may still fail to get a conviction. I think it would be very difficult . . . One doesn't want to muck up what is a strong case by putting in something that's weak.'

A CO cannot punish for indecent assault. He must either acquit if he thinks there is nothing in it, or go for a court martial. Cpl A's CO took Army Legal's advice and went for the court martial. But the offence against Private B, whose evidence appeared the most damning, was not, on Lt. Col. Austin's recommendation, included on the charge sheet. There were six charges in all, two for common assault, four for indecent assault.

The court martial of Cpl A began at 14.00 hrs on 24 October at Colchester.

The court was convened in a low single-storey building, constructed of wood. It had a sad and temporary feel about it. We had expected a much grander building and we wondered whether Cpl A was disappointed that his future was to be decided in something which looked more like an up-market scout hut than a court of law.

He had been looking forward to leaving the Army; instead he now stood before the Judge Advocate. If convicted he could lose his redundancy, his Army pension and his liberty. He sat with his solicitor and listened to a description of what was alleged to have taken place on the night of 23 June 1994.

Over the next five days Lt. Col. Dick Austin, the Army prosecutor, produced a stream of witnesses who testified against Cpl A. Several placed him in the women's accommodation on that night, some remembered him drinking before the alleged incidents, others stated that he had taken contraceptives from his room before going to the women's block.

As the trial wore on – it eventually lasted a full eight days – the evidence, circumstantial though a lot of it was, began to mount against Cpl A. When his turn finally came to take the witness stand on the fifth day, he looked tired but determined to prove his innocence. He was cross-examined by Lt. Col. Austin for over five hours. During all that time he kept his nerve under intense and skilful scrutiny. He always took his time in answering any question and if he was in any doubt about what was meant, he asked for the questions to be repeated. He had a difficult fight on his hands and he was not going to make any silly mistakes. Lt. Col. Austin suggested to him that he was lying and that he had got himself into a situation he could not escape.

Cpl A steadfastly denied that he had done anything wrong and the bench became tired and bored with the contest which was playing out before them. During one of our frequent breaks for a breath of fresh air, the Court Recorder said he thought Cpl A was doing himself no favours whatsoever. He was a veteran of numerous court cases, and his opinion carried considerable weight with those of us gathered in the corridors drinking coffee. He thought that if Cpl A was found guilty the presiding officers would not look kindly upon the fact that he had denied everything and made all the witnesses appear in court to give their evidence. Some of the women who had accused him had found it difficult to describe the events of that night while Cpl A sat across the room from them. Their evident distress brought the proceedings to a halt on more than one occasion.

Mr Richard Porter defended Cpl A. He was a civilian solicitor who practised locally, specializing in Army cases. He made a great deal of Cpl A's unblemished service history and his general good character. He reminded the Court that the 'Golden thread which runs through English law is the presumption that a man is innocent until proven guilty'. He intimated that perhaps the women had behaved as if consent to touch had been given, and that if Cpl A had done anything, it could have been an honest mistake. But if he pushed too hard with his 'honest mistake' defence, it would appear that he accepted Cpl A *had* been there, and was lying after all. He was left with the job of trying to pick holes in the statements of the witnesses.

The case, which had seemed to be heavily weighted against Cpl A, now seemed to be more evenly balanced. As one of the courtroom orderlies remarked, 'I doubt whether we will really get at the truth. It's a balancing act in the end. Those on the bench have to weigh up the evidence on each side and then decide what is most likely to be the truth.'

One thing which did make the whole thing very difficult for the prosecution was the fact that there was no corroborative evidence in any of the incidents. They were left with the circumstantial evidence, the sheer number of witness statements against Cpl A, and his flat denial that he had ever gone anywhere near the women at all. On the eighth day, having listened to all the evidence and the closing speeches of the prosecution and the defence, the Judge Advocate began his summing up. He reviewed all the evidence in a clear and concise way. He drew attention to particular points of law and mapped out the progress of the trial from the first day through to the last. He pointed out the strengths and weaknesses of both cases and he advised the panel of officers on which parts of the evidence were unreliable and should be discarded. Finally, after two hours he asked the President and the two officers to retire to consider their verdict. Cpl A was marched out of the room to wait under guard.

At 12.41 Cpl A was marched back into the courtroom to hear the verdict. He marched slightly slower than he had done in the past and he looked as if the strain was finally getting too much for him.

The President looked at Cpl A and then referred to the note he had in front of him. He began, 'Of the six charges, the Court finds you not guilty of charges Three and Five.' There was a pause whilst Cpl A took it in. 'Of the charge Two there was no finding. Of charges One, Four and Six the Court finds you guilty.'

Cpl A must have been stunned. The charges he had been found guilty of were the indecent assault ones, the worst ones of all. The President said the verdicts were subject to confirmation and asked the escort to march the accused out. Cpl A left in a daze. He had lost; he had been found guilty of a crime he hotly denied, and now his whole future would be in jeopardy.

Afterwards, as people discussed the case, a consensus of what might have happened emerged. If Cpl A had indeed done the things of which he had been accused, it was likely that he had acted under the influence of a quantity of alcohol he was not used to. He had been silly but not malicious, and in each case he had left when it became obvious his attentions were not wanted. If he had admitted it the very next day and apologized, it probably would have gone no further. He may have had a severe reprimand from his CO and that would have been the end of the matter. Unfortunately for him, once the complaints had been made official and the Special Investigation Branch of the Redcaps had become involved, it became difficult to treat the incident as a minor one. During his defence, Mr Porter suggested that the girls had got themselves on to a roller-coaster they could not get off. They all denied that this was the case but, as Mr Porter pointed out, it was not the sort of thing they could admit later, even if they had wanted to. No one felt that Cpl A should get off scot-free if found guilty, but some did think that the whole case had a sad feel about it. A man had been foolish, and the system had propelled everyone along a path few seemed to have much enthusiasm for.

After Cpl A was marched out, Mr Porter made his final plea to the Judge Advocate before the Judge retired to consider the sentence with the board of officers. He repeated his comments about the defendant's good character and unblemished service record. He pointed out that he was buying his house, which might be at risk if he were to lose all means of support, and that a heavy sentence would be crushing to a man in his position. 'Would that be the right way to reward fourteen and a half years of good service for one night of irresponsibility? A heavy sentence would finish him.' He asked the Court to impose a sentence that gave him some sort of future.

After a short while the Court was again in session. Cpl A was recalled to learn his fate. The advising Judge Advocat asked Cpl A if he wanted to call a character witness. This time his reply was quiet and hoarse. He said he did not want to, and he looked the loneliest man in the world. The Judge continued that the sentence was based on the seriousness of the offence and not on the fact that he had pleaded 'not guilty'. He looked at Cpl A before saying he would serve 'One hundred and twelve days in jail and be reduced to the ranks. He would also "soldier on".'

This meant that he would go to jail and lose his redundancy money of £45,000. When he left jail, he would still be in the Army. He would not be able to take up his course at Bristol University, and the house he had in Bristol might well be lost. Cpl A had paid a heavy price for his part in the events of 23 June 1993. The day he was sentenced was 1 November. If nothing had happened on the night of 23 June, that would have been his last contractual day in the Army.

Cpl A was driven the short distance from the Colchester Court Martial Centre to the Military Corrective Training Centre (MCTC) Berechurch Hall Camp – the 'Glasshouse'.

For generations of soldiers (and sailors and airmen as well, for the MCTC is a joint service establishment), the Glasshouse has been an object of abject terror. At best it was believed to be about ten times worse than basic training, at worst dark rumours circulate of savage treatment at the hands of sadistic

NCOs. It is the ultimate punishment, the army Armageddon, where evil prevailed. It is a place to be avoided at all costs.

It is therefore something of a disappointment to see the Glasshouse for the first time. No stocks, no whipping-post, no dungeons, but a low modern complex ('the largest one-storey building in Britain') in pleasant parkland surrounded by trees including 'the oldest oak tree in Essex'. The superlatives stop there. For these are not 'the happiest soldiers in the world'. Indeed, not a few conceal from their nearest and dearest that they are in the MCTC at all, explaining that the capitals stand for 'Motor Cycle Training Centre'. Others simply say they are on an operational tour in Bosnia or Northern Ireland for a while, and therefore incommunicado.

The Colchester Glasshouse (the name probably derives from the military detention centre in Aldershot, which had a conservatory-style roof) was originally neither a 'house' nor 'glass'. It was a tented prisoner-of-war camp established in 1941. The tents were replaced by Nissen huts, which survived until 1988, when todays' building was built.

Spotless turnout and regimental exactitude – part of the Glasshouse way of life.

The Glasshouse is not run by the Redcaps but by a corps that is closely allied, in that it wears an almost identical cap badge, comes under the Provost Marshal, and shares a section of the Redcaps' quarterly in-house magazine. It is called the Military Provost Staff Corps, and is popular with NCOs who want a settled life. Once in the Glasshouse, an Army prison officer will not forever be at the mercy of the posting system. He can buy a house, knowing he will live in it; he can sire a family knowing that his children's education will not be disrupted. These should be the most contented of men, but it has to be said that they present a somewhat sinister appearance in their 'cheese-cutter' hats, which appear to conceal their eyes under a vertical khaki peak. Yet the design is no more than an expedient; a hat with a conventional peak would be knocked off every time an officer put his eye to a judas-hole.

Despite the fact that the Kray twins were at MCTC and were supposed to have made their criminal contacts there, every visitor is told that it is emphatically not a prison. One needs to be constantly reminded of this fact, for to all appearances that is exactly what it is. In some blocks there are cells with barred windows, and soldiers run everywhere under escort. They are locked up at night, and they are not allowed out of the camp, which is ringed with barbed wire. On the other hand, 'Soldiers under Sentence' (SUS) who are trusted use live ammunition on the shooting ranges, and patrol the camp perimeter at night with loaded rifles. It is a place of paradoxes, and given the choice of a civilian gaol, where one can be banged up for twenty-three hours a day, and the Glasshouse, where SUS are subjected to dawn to dusk activity, most people would choose the latter.

Cpl A had no choice. He sits at a desk awaiting admission with several others, in a light high-ceilinged hall that resembles a gym. Around him is his kit. An NCO is sorting through it, putting on one side what Cpl A may keep with him. It is a very small pile. The rest is put into store.

When his name is called, Cpl A stands in front of a staff sergeant who goes through the admission procedure. He is told that his sentence of 112 days will be reduced by a third to 75 days if his behaviour is good. He is given release dates for a remitted and unremitted sentence and then sent off to see the welfare officer, get paid, and join the 200 or so other servicemen under sentence.

Cpl A is paid a starting salary of 57p a day, which makes only a small dent in the £45,000 he has lost. But even this modest per diem is neatly calculated. There will not be much change by the time he has purchased all the cleaning materials he will need to keep up the ferociously high standard required of kit which is inspected minutely and often. But this at least is one area in which the former regimental provost corporal should excel.

Cpl A will spend his time in A Wing. All the servicemen from here will return to their units once they are released. They are a motley crew – mostly Army, but with a sprinkling of sailors and airmen. Their average age is twenty-two and they are in mostly for drugs offences and violence. But there is a third category. One third of the SUS in A Wing were convicted for being Absent Without Leave. In the Army an absentee may find himself in gaol. He will lose his pay. His dependants will suffer (thirteen per cent of A Wing are married). He is guilty not of a crime, but of a military offence.

The regime in A Wing works on the carrot and stick principle, with privileges granted or withheld according to behaviour. As in Dante's 'Inferno', there are different levels of misery in A Wing, calibrated to take account of the serviceman's behaviour. Stage 1 is hyper-regimental with bulled boots, 'boxed' blankets, 'boxed' shirts, ironed newspapers and kit layouts of a Euclidean exactitude. There is no TV, but the shiniest, cleanest, best-swept barrack room (these have eight bed spaces with integral ablutions) may win for itself the privilege of a battered radio, which may go on for a few hours in the evening. Stage 1 SUS are locked up at night.

Promotion to Stage 2 means a payrise from 57p to 82p per day, plus a black-and-white television and an unlocked door at night. Stage 3 SUS earn £1.96 a day; they have colour television and access to a phone.

The aim of the Glasshouse is to return SUS to their units as better soldiers: fitter, more efficient, abler at their job, and more highly motivated. So they get up at six and it is lights out at ten, and the hours in between are unrelieved activity – marching, running, crossing assault courses, Swedish drills with heavy logs, and plunging bayonets into sacks of straw while uttering blood-curdling screams. These are not on the whole hardened criminals; they are a living commercial for the efficiency of the 'short sharp shock'.

There are three other wings. F Wing is for females; and is much smaller than the men's blocks, because females are on the whole better behaved than males. C Wing is a high-security prison within a prison designed for servicemen who are in serious trouble. The Glasshouse will not accommodate offenders whose sentences exceed two years, so servicemen in C Wing are either awaiting trial on grave charges or waiting for confirmation of long court martial sentences before leaving the

The Glasshouse soldiers under sentence' (SUS) are deployed to the day's fatigues – cleaning the sergeants' mess, the officers' mess, etc.

Glasshouse to begin serving time in a civilian gaol. There are seven cells in C Wing equipped with washing and toilet facilities. When we visited, one cell was occupied by a service dependant awaiting trial accused of murder at the British military base in Rheindahlen (who has since been sentenced to be detained at Her Majesty's Pleasure at a General Court Martial held in Germany).

D Wing is roughly the same size as A Wing, but D Wing is for the servicemen the services want to boot out. When they have done their time in D Wing, they are discharged. There is no love lost between A and D Wings. A-Wingers would like to leave, but have to soldier on: at least forty per cent of D Wingers want to stay on, but have to go. Civilian life frightens them. In D Wing thirty-nine per cent were there on drug offences, twenty-five per cent for being Absent Without Leave, eighteen per cent for crimes of dishonesty, and fourteen per cent for violence.

In the Glasshouse they try to teach these servicemen on discharge some basic skills. There are workshops where they can learn bricklaying, carpentry, painting and decorating, and car maintenance. Half a mile from the main complex, away from the screaming of sergeants and echoey bawling of physical training instructors is – a pig unit. Here the inoculation and breeding programme is in the hands of SUS.

As part of an acclimatization to civilian life, Stage 3 D-Wingers are allowed into Colchester unescorted and in civilian clothes. But God help them if they are found in a pub. Discovery would lead to an immediate loss of all their hard-earned privileges. There is no doubt that many soldiers find the enforced discharge into civilian society a terrifying prospect. They know no other life than the Army: it feeds them, clothes them, pays them and houses them – both them and their families. Outside the Army is a hostile world of unemployment and housing shortage. The D-Winger spends a lot of time learning how to sign on for the baffling array of DSS handouts, how to find a job, how to get help with rent, how to cope . . .

On the day that he bids farewell to the Glasshouse, each D Wing serviceman is presented with a presentation pack of leaflets called 'Where do I go from here?' It is full of complex reading on DSS regulations, and courses run

Lt. Col. Richard Austin, a distinguished soldier, then a civilian barrister, now in charge of all military legal matters in Eastern Command.

by the Department of Employment. To compound the misery, the Health Education Authority chips in with 'That's the limit – a guide to sensible drinking', 'The facts about HIV and AIDS' and the 'Guide to a healthy sex life'. Finally, when it has all got too much, there is 'Nowhere to turn? – it helps to talk about it,' issued by the Samaritans.

Whether Cpl A was feeling suicidal when he left the Glasshouse with full remission for good behaviour is not known. It *is* known that he felt exceedingly bitter. For one night of irresponsibility – and he still pleaded his innocence – he was ruined.

Prima facie, the court martial decision that Cpl A should 'soldier on' seemed cruel. In fact the court had reached the decision at the express request of Cpl A's defending solicitor, Richard Porter.. If he had been thrown out of the Army, the redundancy payment would automatically have been lost. As it is, there is a scintilla of hope in the form of an appeal.

Cpl A's court martial took so long because Lt. Col. Dick Austin for the Army and Richard Porter for the defendant were locked in legal argument. Austin wanted all the charges tried together, arguing that they were all linked. But Porter wanted the six charges tried separately, arguing that the evidence could easily have been concocted by the victims and witnesses among themselves. The Judge Advocate supported Austin, so the charges were all heard together. But a Court of Appeal might not be of the same opinion as the Judge Advocate.

At some time in the future two cases will come before the Law Lords, which will determine whether Cpl A can keep his £45,000. The first is R.*v.* Ananthanarayanan, in which a consultant psychiatrist was convicted for indecent assaults on various nurses. As with Cpl A, the charges were heard together. The Court of Appeal threw out the verdict on the grounds that the evidence may not have been independent. The House of Lords will deliver a final judgement on the issue. The second case is R.*v.*'H' involving a stepfather's indecent assault on his stepdaughter and others. If the House of Lords rules that in multiple cases of indecent assault the evidence for all the charges taken together is unsafe, then Cpl A's appeal could be successful.

Cpl A will not appeal until the House of Lords has spoken, and the matter will then grind through the military appeals procedure. First it will be placed before the Army Board, and finally the Courts Martial Appeal Court.

If Cpl A is successful, the verdict will be quashed. The clock will immediately revert to the *status quo ante*, to the position he was in before the guilty verdict was pronounced at the court martial. He will be a substantive corporal again, receiving full corporal's pay, awaiting a redundancy payment of £45,000 after fourteen and a half blameless years in the British Army. Then there will be a question of compensation: a university place he could not take up; a mortgage he has lost; three months unjust imprisonment in the Glasshouse.

It is a big 'if', and, whatever happens, it is going to be a long, long wait.

CHAPTER 9

ROLE IN COMBAT

The RMP support the Army in a combat role. They are responsible for the control and movement of all troops and their supporting paraphernalia during a conflict. This means they have to go with the first wave of troops.

Since many attacks start with large quantities of troops parachuting into a new front, the RMP has its own parachute unit – Para Provost. Para Provost jump with the minimum of kit. Their job is to establish a network of routes and sign-post them so that the main body of soldiers that follow will know which way to go. Obviously, it would be disastrous if the main body of men struck out in the wrong direction. In battle, when chaos seems to reign it is essential that soldiers can find the battle front and logistic support can find their muster stations. This is dangerous and vital work; without it, chaos would indeed precede certain defeat.

Para Provost – 'first in, last out'.

The men of Para Provost have maps, signs and a weapon; they must establish where the routes are and erect their signs so they are visible to everyone. They establish control-points at crossroads and junctions, and they man these to control the flow of traffic. History is littered with battles won and lost because soldiers and their supporting resources were bogged down in a log-jam of people and equipment on the way to a battle front. It is the job of the RMP to make sure this does not happen to the British Army.

Once a network has been established, the RMP move forward with the advance troops, signposting the way for the rest to follow. During the Gulf War, one American general, desperate to be the first on Kuwaiti soil, took his armoured personnel carrier forward to a bridge. On the other side Kuwait beckoned. He charged across to reclaim the country for the Allies, only to discover an advance party of RMP were already there and pointing him in the direction of the capital. The general was furious; glorious advances do not look so good when they encounter a traffic policeman standing by the side of the road to make sure they don't get lost.

An advance party must do everything within its power

The RMP have to control the traffic and point the way to the battle front in times of war. In this exercise, the Royal Engineers had to get an entire division across a river. They built this pontoon in three minutes.

to help maintain the momentum of a full-scale attack. During the Gulf War SSgt Kevin Davies commanded 3 Platoon, 203 Provost Company, which was advancing with the 7th Armoured Brigade. The brigade had breached a line of defences and SSgt Davies and his men were required to go forward along-side the armoured reconnaissance to lay out the route for the rest of the brigade.

He was given the task of finding a route, and then advancing to a 'forming up point' or FUP. Once established, the main body of the brigade would arrive and occupy it, and from there logistical support would be organized to supply the forward elements of the advance which were now some four hours ahead. It became imperative that this was done quickly, otherwise the forward element's rate of advance would falter without the proper support, and the advance would lose momentum.

However, when SSgt Davies and his men arrived at the FUP they found that it contained numerous Multi-Launch Rocket System bomblets: in other words, it was a minefield. Within a short time three soldiers had been wounded and one killed, and SSgt Davies' own platoon had lost one Landrover and a motorbike to the bombs. By the time they had sorted themselves out, darkness had fallen and, of all things, it started to rain, making visibility almost nil.

The rest of the brigade were still heading to the FUP and at that moment it was impassable. SSgt Davies was ordered to clear a safe lane to allow the rest of the brigade to form up and support the advance. SSgt Davies personally led his men forward to clear a path through the bomblets. Since there was no time to lose they had to use the only equipment available – Army issue shovels. Despite an early explosion which miraculously injured no one, S/Sgt Davies and his men continued to work forwards clearing a way for some 600 vehicles to pass through.

They had worked around the clock to forge the route, and during the following days they continued to do the same, despite the fact that the platoon became increasingly tired and stressed. For his exemplary personal courage and robust leadership, SSgt Kevin Davies was awarded the Distinguished

Conduct Medal (DCM).

SSgt Davies comes from a long line of RMP heroes. During the First World War the corps won 13 Distinguished Service Medals, 8 Military Crosses, 65 Distinguished Conduct Medals, 260 Military Medals, 26 Meritorious Medals, 105 mentions in despatches – and they lost 375 men.

In the RMP museum at their Training Centre in Chichester there is a room which measures approximately twelve feet by eight. It is completely full of campaign medals won by members of the RMP. One of the Distinguished Conduct Medals was won by WO1 Glenister who was the Regimental Sergeant Major for 102 Provost Company during the evacuation of Dunkirk in the Second World War: 'At dusk on Saturday 1 June 1940, after being engaged for three days and nights in embarkation duties at Bray Dunnes during continuous heavy bombing and shelling WO1 Glenister assisted in the removal of the wounded, frequently under heavy fire, until he was ordered to embark at 21:00 hrs – whereas he could have left at 10:00hrs that day. During the whole period and whilst under heavy bombing and shelling he carried out reconnaissance, traffic and embarkation duties with ability. By his coolness and devotion to duty he set a fine example to the men under him and contributed greatly to the successful withdrawal and embarkation of the British troops'. WO1 Glenister was also awarded a Bronze Star by the Americans for his involvement with them in the later stages of the war.

For the RMP, perhaps what is most significant about this story is the fact that it reminds people that their claim to be the 'first in and last out' is not a hollow boast. By virtue of their job they must be 'first in' to sign the way forward and 'last out' to sign the retreat. By far the largest proportion of RMP casualties during both world wars have been sustained carrying out this duty.

In the First World War the Commander-in-Chief's last despatch read: 'In the battle zone where they did duty in exposed positions under heavy fire and suffered severe casualties, they solved an important part of the problem of traffic control by preventing the unavoidable congestion of troops and transport on roads in the vicinity of active operations – and prevented the situation from degenerating into confusion.'

In the Second World War their casualties numbered 917. They won 229 operational awards, amongst which were 7 Military Crosses, 6 Distinguished Conduct Medals, 61 Military Medals and 776 mentions in despatches. They earned a reputation for bravery and devotion to duty, and were present on every battlefield and in every country where British troops fought.

General Sir Myles Dempsey KCB KCB DSO paid the following tribute: 'The military policeman became so well known a figure on every road to the battlefield that his presence became taken for granted. Few soldiers as they hurried over a bridge, which was a regular target for the enemy, gave much thought to the man whose duty it was to be there for hours on end directing the traffic and ensuring its rapid passage.'

In 1946, in recognition of their outstanding war record, HM King George VI granted the Military Police a royal prefix; thereafter they became the Royal Military Police.

Since the Second World War the RMP seem to have been as busy as ever. They have served in every operational theatre: the occupation of Germany, conflicts in Korea, Cyprus, Aden, Borneo, the list goes on. More recently,

SSgt Kevin Davies receives his DSM from the Queen.

they have policed the army in Rhodesia, the Falklands and, of course, the Gulf and Bosnia.

Although every regiment likes to trumpet its heroes and triumphs, the RMP are keenly aware that such highs come out of many, many lows, or as one old RSM put it: 'Long hours, long days of doing the same thing no matter how boring, attention to detail always; that's why we command the respect we do – because we can do it.' Doing the basics, keeping it simple, never cutting corners is the way they are trained at Chichester, and the way they have always been trained. No matter how mind-numbingly tedious it may be, the Military Policeman will always be at his post doing his duty.

During both world wars one of the most boring and at the same time vital parts of the MP's job was the thankless task of the 'pointsman'. The pointsman was the poor unfortunate that manned every important junction or crossroads on the field of operations and whose task it was to 'point' all troops and transport in the right direction. This job was one of those tasks which was a mixture of real and present danger and long hours of repetitive monotony. Because he was 'pointing' troops to the front the pointsman was often close enough to be the target of shelling or sniper fire. However, for long periods there would be little danger and the job would become mundane. In the Second World War, 3,000 military policemen guided 25,000 vehicles to their stations.

For the most part, the job itself was fairly straightforward: troops were sent to the front, supplies to the depots and the ordnance to the weapon stores. However, occasionally things would liven up a little: for example, new pointsmen always seemed to underestimate the stopping distance of a tank, and this invariably resulted in a never-to-be-forgotten lesson.

Most of them spent their time in uncomfortable locations with the minimum of home comforts and atrocious weather. However, they did have their good days. In the RMP museum there is an old photograph of two pointsmen in Arnhem. They are 'pointing' the way to the bridge and they are both pictured in glorious sunshine sitting in two padded armchairs, relaxing as if they had not a care in the world (see page 106).

This would not be the case for their mobile counterparts. The RMP also provided pointsmen on motorbikes. These men often drew the attention of the enemy snipers as they moved forward with the main advances. As if that was not enough, they also had to contend with decapitation wire traps along their new routes. After a number of particularly nasty casualties the RMP and the Army in general started fitting a wire-cutting attachment on to the front of most of their bikes. This took the shape of an angled piece of metal welded to the front. It was slanted slightly backwards so that if it did not cut the wire it would force it up and over the rider who crouched behind.

In the Second World War, the mobile pointsman became very important to the Army. He could move much more speedily and over greater distances when directed by a mobile pointsman working ahead. Because of this it was often the RMP pointsman on his motorbike who was the first soldier to 'liberate' many of the European cities during the Allied advance. Although the RMP would never claim to be the first into Berlin they do have an old photograph which shows two pointsmen astride their machines in what looks to be a very deserted capital city.

If the pointsman was a familiar sight throughout the battlefields of the Second World War, then the RMP's signs must have seemed like part of the furniture. Every turning or junction that needed traffic directing through it, but did not merit the presence of RMP personnel, got a whole batch of signs. These signs had to be clear, simple and durable. The RMP decided to manufacture the signs themselves. After some experimentation they created a route sign that was as 'squaddie proof' as it was possible to produce.

They were called Franco plates and were made of heavy sheet metal. They could take a fair amount of punishment, could survive being hit by lorries and run over by tanks. The only thing the RMP could not do was make them theft-proof. Since a fair number always went missing, all pointsmen had a stencil kit available so they could knock up a new sign on the spot.

In fact, the ability to produce durable signs quickly as a situation dictates contributed significantly to the success of numerous operations on the battlefield. At one point during the Second World War, the RMP had a sign-making 'factory' at Antwerp where scores of corps personnel managed to produce nearly 6,000 signs in five months.

Out on the ground, if there are no steel plates available, the RMP corporal was expected to improvise. This took many forms: petrol cans were often used as well as conveniently placed trees and rocks. One night-time design involved the use of a four-gallon can which was punched with holes using a hammer and nail. The holes made up the letters of the sign with an arrow along the bottom. A light was then put inside, to shine through the holes illuminating the words. It was cheap, durable and weather proof.

At El Alamein, RMP pointsmen used night-time lights to direct troops and tanks through its minefields. They marked the edges of the minefields with red and green lamps and despite the constant wash of sand from the vehicles managed to keep them all working long enough to allow the convoys to pass through. Although this story may seem hardly worth reporting, it does demonstrate the fact that even a small task done well can be invaluable in the right circumstances. The fact that the RMP could always be trusted to carry out a large but often laborious set of tasks quickly and efficiently became increasingly important to the officers and commanders on the ground. 'Despite such laborious signing of routes the presence of military police to direct control and reassure columns of troops and vehicles did much to ensure their safe and orderly advance to their objectives.'

Of course the RMP were one group amongst many who did a good job and did their duty. What makes them different is the fact that today, fifty years on from the battlefields of Europe, they are exactly the same. They have the same standards, the same straightforward uncomplicated view of the world and the same dedication to their work.

Being drawn into the RMP of today is like being part of a club that still deals with the values and perspectives of the past. Instead of being a disadvantage, this above all else is their greatest strength. From SSgt Kevin Davies

*Arnhem, Second World War.
RMP pointsmen take a rare
break from their duties.*

in the Gulf who took a shovel and cleared the path through the minefield to the men and women who conscientiously carry out a million mundane tasks, the motivation is the same: *Exemplo Ducemus* - by example shall we lead. It is a real statement of purpose and identity.

In Bosnia the RMP is present in its usual function as the policemen of the British soldiers serving with the UN. However, they also have their wartime function of supply-route work. For the former republic of Yugoslavia this is particularly important, since the supply routes have become the only real life-line there is for some areas.

The corps patrol the routes, stop, search and check vehicles at the various vehicle check points. They also brief all UN traffic on the route ahead, what the weather conditions will be, where the fighting is and what kind of dangers they are likely to face. This enables the RMP to monitor most of the movements of the UN transport and keep their headquarters up to date with the positions of their trucks and personnel.

When a new battalion arrives, the RMP are in a position to escort them on their first patrols, showing them the lie of the land and helping them to get settled in. They also escort some of the convoys that take aid through, and they are often harassed and looted on parts of their journey. If one particular aid agency is being targeted, the RMP will escort that convoy for a time to discourage further attacks. They never allow a convoy to stop since this often results in the local population swarming over the trucks and stripping the convoy bare.

The RMP spend a great deal of time liaising with the warring factions that man the various road-blocks. By keeping a good working relationship with the opposing soldiers the corps succeed in getting many more convoys through than might otherwise make it. One particular black spot where convoys are often stopped and stripped is called 'Bon Bon corner', so-called because the children who swarm out to meet the convoy all call out for sweets.

When they are not escorting convoys a large amount of RMP effort goes into combating theft from UN stores and the resulting black market that it supplies. Trading between the locals and the fighting soldiers as well as between the opposing sides themselves is fairly widespread.

They are also tasked with the extremely difficult job of gathering evidence of war crimes. The RMP are considered the nearest thing there is to 'international police' in Bosnia and so have the unenviable task of accumulating evidence against those accused of committing atrocities.

They have a considerable caseload on which to work. One involves three UN people who were held up on a road before being marched down to the banks of a nearby river. One was then shot in the back of the head, and the other two were shot in the back as they dived into the river. Both survived and swam to safety. The RMP are investigating the case.

They are also completing a case for the Italian Government who asked them to investigate the murder of five of its citizens in 1993. This kind of work is not new to the RMP. They have already done the same in Kuwait, where the invading Iraqi army has been reported to have carried out various crimes against humanity. For the most part the men and women on the ground would much prefer not to be involved in conflicts of this kind but they do a job most other countries are ill-equipped to deal with.

The corps' involvement with other governments is not always so grim. They undertake a fair number of escort duties when visiting dignitaries come to Britain. In 1953, during the coronation, they escorted the colourful Queen Salote of Tonga. Back in 1918 the NCOs who escorted the Austrian Emperor into exile each received a gold watch for their services. More recently, RMPs were involved in security operations during the wedding of Lady Diana Spencer and Prince Charles.

British Government officials have also taken advantage of an RMP escort. Harold Macmillan took one with him whenever he visited Moscow, and our ambassador in Vietnam had a permanent one towards the end of that war. RMP escorts are also used for prisoner duties. During the First World War they escorted prisoners-of-war whenever they had to be moved or transported. They also escorted our own prisoners if they had been sentenced to death by a military court martial. The long walk to the firing squad was invariably in the company of the RMP, and if the execution was not a clean one it was the duty of the RMP officer present to administer the final bullet with his pistol.

The RMP has many responsibilities during war, some are dangerous, some unpleasant and some plain tedious, but they are all carried out to the letter: *Exemplo Ducemus.*

Bosnia. An RMP Landrover, painted United Nations white, patrols a village near Vitez, scene of ethnic cleansing.

CHAPTER *10*

BANG BANG – YOU'RE DEAD

There is a group of people in the RMP who are kept out of the public eye as much as possible. They do not appear on the news, in the papers or on the television. If you were to ring the RMP to enquire about them you would be politely rebuffed. They are the RMP bodyguards, the corps élite, the men and women of the Close Protection Unit.

Their job is to protect high-ranking members of the armed forces from terrorist attack. They also protect members of the Government and the royal family when they travel abroad. They are resident in most British embassies where there is any kind of perceived threat to the ambassador or his family. These are serious people. They shun any kind of publicity and will go to a great deal of trouble to keep out of the limelight. Inquisitive journalists are discouraged and the investigative journalist sold a bum steer. They are not mentioned in print, rarely photographed and they do not feature in the Sunday supplements.

When we started researching the corps for the TV series, we were told about the CP unit. The RMP is proud of it and, after a few initial misgivings, decided that they could be included in the series. There was a barrow-load of provisos attached, but at least we were going to be allowed to film the secretive world of the 'CP operative'.

However, when production finally got under way things changed. The Ministry of Defence had intervened and the CP Unit was off the agenda. A series of explanations were given, the last being that the procedures they use were too sensitive to be publicized, we would put people's lives at risk and, once their procedures were made public, they would have to start again. Despite assurances from us that we would not compromise anyone's security, and despite a planned security viewing where the RMP and the Army could check we had not crossed the line, we were still told we could not include CP in the series. After giving the series approval a full year before, someone in the Ministry of Defence had got cold feet. However now along with the book comes a new opportunity to include the CP Unit and this time we did not have to ask the Ministry of Defence for permission.

(Opposite, above) A Close Protection team and their 'protectee', General Sir Peter de la Billiere, somewhere in the Gulf.

(Opposite, below) Close Protection establish an inner protection circle around an ambassador's car.

109

What follows has been written with a great deal of care. We would not wish to compromise any individual's safety or the RMP's procedures. This is done willingly to protect those who spoke to us and not to pander to the neuroses of the MoD.

The Close Protection Unit is a highly disciplined part of the RMP. Operatives are isolated from the rest of the corps, tucked away in a quiet corner of southern England where they are more than happy to let the rest of the world pass by. They have their own rules and procedures, and they tend to keep themselves to themselves.

If you visited their main training establishment, you would immediately become aware of the fact that these people do not fall into the accepted stereotype of bodyguards. They do not seek to glamorize themselves, they do not strut about in a pair of dark sunglasses looking mean and brooding. In fact, one of the most striking things about meeting them is that they are terribly nice. They will make an effort to sound interested in what you have to say, even if it bores them to tears. The reason? It is all part of their training. These people move in circles where they must blend in. At an ambassador's cocktail party they would look a little daft doing a Kevin Costner number. The CP pride themselves on being the 'invisible deterrent'. They are always there, but we would find it hard to pick them out. They do not march alongside a VIP looking all Armani and hair gel. Instead, they are more likely to be tagging along as an insignificant aide or even a reporter.

Next time you see a news item showing Sir 'Head of Troops' or Sir 'Head of Boats' visiting another country, look closely at the people nearest to him. If there is a person you immediately discount as being his or her bodyguard, then you are probably looking at him. If the shot is wide enough for you to see the crowd, look at them carefully as well. There you have 'Sir Boats' strutting his stuff, the centre of attention with all eyes on his every move. In the crowd there will be quite a few pairs of eyes ignoring 'Sir Boats' altogether; they will be looking in the opposite direction, firmly fixed on the crowd itself, watching for a possible assassin.

Playing 'Spot the BG' is a favourite game in the security world. We have yet to meet anyone in it who does not claim to be an expert. In the same way that everyone claims to be a driver of 'above average' standard, so every spook in the world claims he can spot a BG a mile off. However, some BGs are better than others. The bodyguards of the CP unit seem to be better at watching, better at blending in, perhaps just better at doing the job than anyone else around. The RMP Close Protection Unit have been unofficially voted the best in the world by those who vote with their feet and their wallets and pay to have their bodyguards trained 'the right way', the RMP way.

The RMP training course is extremely popular with other governments, and nervous politicians around the world who are keen for their personal bodyguards to have the best training available. After all, it's one of the few jobs where an employee cannot afford to learn by his mistakes: 'Sorry boss, next time I will check the car for booby-traps . . .'

The course instructors talk about mistakes a lot. They may even be obsessed. 'In this job we cannot afford them. You must understand that this is the only profession in the world where making one small mistake can cost the man next to you his life. That's why we put so much into the training, we have to make sure we do it the best way possible.'

That way revolves around a dedication to saving the 'protectee' in the event of a terrorist attack. Everything else is subjugated to this goal, training is thorough and extensive. The courses are long and demanding and, although a high level of fitness is essential for the job, the right mental attitude is deemed to be far more important. The RMP do not want any gung-ho types. If students display too much of a liking for the weapons side they become the focus of a lot of extra attention. The instructors watch for a tendency to 'shoot it out' John Wayne style, and those that cannot curb such inclinations are binned.

They want people who can think and operate under stress, and have the ability to think rationally when all hell breaks loose: 'It's no good being super-alert, having lightning reflexes and then being the first person to move in the wrong direction. That way, you are just the fastest guy to get to the morgue. You have got to assess and calculate while everyone else runs around like headless chickens. That way you are the first guy out of trouble and the first guy to get bought a drink by a grateful ambassador.'

Close Protection operatives constantly scan the surrounding crowd and keep close to their high-ranking protectee. If anyone were to throw a bomb or grenade, both operatives would be expected to cover the officer and protect his life with their bodies.

The CP provide protection for ambassadors in any country where there is a perceived threat. Each embassy has its own particular set of problems. The CP Unit that flies out to combat that threat will already have 'lived' in the embassy before they actually set foot in it. At their training base in England there are houses which are entirely dedicated to reproducing the environment that the unit can expect to find when they actually reach the job. It would be no good a unit turning up and being completely unfamiliar with the layout of the embassy and its grounds. Local terrorists are not going to give them a few days 'to settle in' before mounting an operation.

As one source put it, 'You have to get off the plane and be ready, instantly. Suppose it's your first day in the embassy and you get hit. You rush the ambassador to the nearest exit – away from the danger. You pick the nearest door, only problem is you all pile into the broom cupboard. You end up dead or you are trying to explain how he bought it amongst the mops and the Vim. Either way you go straight to gaol and you do not pass Go.'

The CP call anyone they are protecting the 'protectee'. Rushing the protectee away from the source of danger is a good illustration of the priorities of the CP. Standing there and shooting it out would not be a rational course of action; the priority is to protect and if that means a withdrawal from the scene then that is what is done. No one worries about this being a 'retreat'. If they save the protectee from harm they have won, that is their job.

One of the first things a CP operative does on visiting any new location is look for the ways of leaving it. Exits are of great importance to the effective bodyguard, 'routes out' are explored and memorized. If there was an attack, a CP operative must be able to bundle their charge away from danger instantly they must always know which way to go – instantly.

At the training centre there are a wide variety of locations where they can practise their techniques. There are real streets with real houses along which the trainees can test their newly-acquired skills. Admittedly, the houses do not contain any residents and they seem a little forlorn, but this is mainly due to the fact that the entire neighbourhood is riddled with bullet holes and every other window has been smashed and burned out. There are sections which represent built-up areas and there are sections that represent suburbia. There are A roads and B roads, country roads, lanes and woods – in fact there is just about any environment the CP operative is likely to have to work in. Describing it as an SAS playground may be a little far-fetched but it certainly felt like that when we were there. Every so often there was the distant rattle of automatic fire and the odd crump of something heavier and nastier.

On one occasion we were walking through the woods section when two very hot and heavily-laden Gurkhas appeared on the track ahead. They ran up and asked us where a particular bridge was. They were doing an orienteering test, and asking wandering film producers the way comes under the 'initiative' bit. In the event we were actually able to send them off in the right direction. Later that day, in another part of the training complex, we watched the Unit garage and workshop being used as a useful location for an exercise. A group of trainees BGs were escorting a' VIP' through the building when they came under 'attack'. The purpose of the exercise was to test the trainee's response to a fairly heavy assault in a location where their options for escape were limited. They took the only sensible exit available, through the back of the garage. This was fine but, once outside, they chose the wrong direction for a complete get-away and got 'riddled' on the spot.

In reality, there are always enough CP operatives around with enough firepower to fight off any large and determined assault, but their priority will always be to get the 'protectee' away from the danger. On some occasions they will have to stand and 'neutralize the threat', and then the CP's considerable talent for 'laying down a field of fire' would come into play.

Whilst with the CP, we watched some weapons training and were surprised by the sheer volume of ordnance that could be expended in such a short time. When we questioned someone about it, the rather obvious but nevertheless brutal reality of a 'fire fight' was explained to us. 'When this situation occurs there is only one way to survive: you have to hit first and hard. It's not like in the movies where the firing seems to go on for ages and half the shots miss. In reality they don't.'

As for the question of courage in these situations, the RMP have a novel way for finding out if a person is made of the 'right stuff'. This is important since in their line of work they may be required to make the ultimate sacrifice and 'stop a bullet'. BGs around the world are often nicknamed 'bullet catchers'. All the trainees are brought together for a spot of 'milling'. Milling is all about bottle. The trainees are put in twos and each pair is given an oversized pair of boxing gloves - oversized so that they are a little unwieldy, and the power of a punch is lessened, cutting down on serious injuries. The trainees are now expected to 'show real aggression'. It is all about courage and character, and those that cannot let fly or those that shrink away from an onslaught are usually the ones the RMP do not want.

When they are not knocking six bells out of each other, the new trainees are given another way to get the adrenalin flowing. The skid-pan is a very large area of flat tarmac where they learn the art of anti-terrorist driving techniques. It is a boy-racer's paradise. Here the trainees abuse cars and make them do things they were not designed for. The car-casualty rate is very high but the end result is worth it.

During the war in Lebanon in the early 1980s a CP unit was escorting a 'protectee' from A to B. As the vehicles moved into one particular area, a threat appeared in the form of a car full of armed gunmen which began following the small convoy. The unit let them get close enough to assess the degree of threat, before deciding on a course of action. The gunmen were encouraged to try and pass the CP car. The CP moved aside and the driver of the gunmen took the bait and moved forward. Once they were level they did not stay that way for long: the CP driver swung his wheel and drove the gunmen's car into the ditch. They disappeared in a storm of astonished faces, smashing glass and swirling dust.

For the CP Unit it was another win – the protectee was safe and the threat had been removed. There had been no shoot-out or car chase, instead a calm assessment of the situation and a course of action chosen which would render most protection to the VIP; no heroics, just calculated professionalism.

If questioned about their successes, most CPs will say they are due to the quality of their 'training': 'Train, train and then train again just in case.' The fact that this works and is not just a mindless slogan is borne out by another incident which occurred in Beruit in 1984. On Thursday 20 September at eleven in the morning the British ambassador arrived at the American embassy for a meeting with his counterpart.

The British ambassador was accompanied by a CP team who deployed to their set positions upon his arrival. Both ambassadors then went up to the fourth floor of the building to begin the meeting. Forty minutes later a van appeared at the gates of the embassy. It contained 2,000 lb of high explosives and it was driven by a suicide bomber. When he failed to bluff his way past the guards at the gate, the bomber accelerated forward towards the embassy. The plan had been to head straight for the underground car park where he would detonate the bomb. The whole building would have collapsed, killing the majority of its occupants.

CP operatives make their last checks before allowing the protectee ambassador to leave the safety of his residence and head for his car.

As the vehicle raced forwards, the guards at the gate managed to fire a few shots as it sped away from them, but to no effect. The attack would have been successful had it not been for the presence of Cpl 'Smith' of the CP team protecting the British ambassador. He was stationed outside the building and within sight of the front gates. He had noticed the van when it had arrived and had kept a close watch on it as the driver argued with the guards. When it suddenly sped towards the building he was able to react almost instantly. He shouldered his HK53 assault rifle and fired five times into the driver's cab. The driver slumped to one side and the van veered off its course, swerved into a parked car and exploded.

Cpl 'Smith' was thrown thirty feet by the blast. Inside the building on the fourth floor some of the structure gave way and the American ambassador was pinned beneath a large piece of concrete. He was freed by another CP operative and the British ambassador.

Outside, Cpl 'Smith' who was suffering from 'blast deafness', managed to organize the emergency services as they tried to reach the injured. In total, eight people died in the blast, and many more were injured. Had it not been for the presence of the Close Protection Unit the death toll would have been in the hundreds.

This kind of attention to detail and instant reaction comes from training. During research for the series we spent a day watching a new group of CP trainees being put through their paces in a mid-term test. The test involved a 'protectee' being escorted by the trainees around a course that had been designed to throw all sorts of surprises at them. The head of the training course played the part of the ambassador, and the course instructors played various terrorists who were to attack the unit as they moved around with their precious charge. The trainees had absolutely no idea when or where the attacks would come from, how strong they would be or the kind of weapons that would be used against them.

Although everyone involved knew this to be no more than a dummy run, the tension was considerable. A serious mistake here would put a question mark over a particular person, as the RMP want only those who will react in the right way. Lose your cool and you do not become part of the CP. The other thing that contributed to the high level of stress felt by those being scrutinized was the fact that the 'attackers' would be firing real terrorist weapons, admittedly only loaded with blanks, but if you have ever been close enough to a machine-gun that is spewing out blanks you do not really care that it is not quite the real thing – it feels like it!

During the preparations, we noticed the odd grin and a certain amount of masochistic anticipation among the instructors who were to play the terrorists. 'We want to make it as realistic as possible, don't we?' said one, lovingly oiling a nasty-looking rocket-launcher.

Of the actual event itself there is little we can report in detail that would not cause a problem for someone, but the resulting expenditure of blanks and pyrotechnics makes the toughest of those fake war-games look like a stroll in the park with Noddy and Big Ears.

One incident which is reportable is the extent to which the instructors go to make the trainees understand they must always be prepared for the 'unexpected'. It was towards the end of the test, and what had gone on before had left quite a few of the trainees looking a shade rattled and nervous. Now they were to escort their 'protectee' around an imaginary car salesroom. Two cars had been placed side by side and the 'terrorists' had set their trap.

Putting trainees in situations they are likely to encounter on the job is an important part of the course. As one instructor explained, 'Ambassadors are renowned for not liking the constraints of having a BG following them everywhere and some will make a point of not allowing the fact to interefere with what they feel should be an ordinary life. One ambassador collected butterflies and would often go off with his net chasing about in all sorts of undesirable places. The CP with him just had to do the best they could and try not to tread on the rare ones.'

On the test, the trainees drove their VIP to the showroom and deployed as per their training. They looked extremely nervous and kept their weapons within easy reach at all times. A 'salesman' greeted the VIP and showed him the first of the two cars. His patter was actually quite good and the VIP looked suitably impressed. However, after a little thought he decided he wanted to see something else. He was then taken across to the second car which was much bigger and more to his liking. The salesman went into overdrive and even the closest BG began to get interested in the marvellous attributes of the car on offer.

By now the salesman and the VIP were standing at the rear of the car admiring the very large back bumper. At the very second the closest BG looked down at the bumper, the boot flew open and a man with a mask opened up with a machine-gun at point-blank range. The noise was deafening, and time did indeed seem to stand still. The BG appeared to take off. One second he was standing looking at the bumper, the next he was in the air trying to bring his gun down to bear on the attacker. To his credit, by the time he was on the way down again he had his gun out and was firing back at the 'terrorist'. Others flashed towards the VIP and he was bundled back into the car.

Since the VIP was actually the man who ran the course, I assumed there would be some harsh words said afterwards, not least because as they pushed him back into the car they managed to crack his head against the door pillar.

When we later asked him about the rough treatment he gave a world-weary shrug; it was not the physical injury he minded so much as the heavy toll these exercises took on his clothes. Certainly, looking at him at the very end of the test he did look as though he had been dragged through a hedge backwards.

'We do train them to be as careful as they can – but when it comes down to it you just have to do what's necessary to get the person moving. Quite often, close gunfire will make a lot of people freeze. They are rooted to the spot for a few seconds. We cannot afford to wait for them to move, so sometimes we have to do the moving regardless of the dignity of someone like an ambassador. Anyway, afterwards they would be fairly grateful, I would think.'

The lesson certainly seemed to have been learned by the trainees. They checked every space that could conceivably conceal a human being thereafter and treated every door as if it had a man with a machine-gun behind it.

At the end of the test the trainees all trooped off for yet another lecture. This time the subject was how to cope with the problems of living cheek-by-jowl with an ambassador and his family and not get on everyone's nerves. It seems that tact and diplomacy were as large a part of being a CP operative as weapon-handling and advanced driving. Being a bodyguard in the RMP is not a simple matter at all. The successful ones are resourceful, cool, multi-talented individuals who do quite a complicated job – not like the movies, not Kevin Costnerish at all.

CHAPTER *11*

NORTHERN IRELAND

It is difficult to ignore Northern Ireland. Until recently, over two-thirds of the corps' strength has been based in the Province. It was intended that it should be included in the television series; the RMP actually suggested it first and arranged for us to visit and research the subject.

Although there were obvious and understandable security concerns, the corps were keen we should see at least some of the work they do 'across the water'. The Northern Ireland Office were not quite so keen, however. They listened to our reassurances and protestations of 'good intentions', and then a week before we were due to start filming pulled the plug on the whole thing.

When we asked for an explanation, we were told that Northern Ireland was 'too sensitive at the moment'. We often wondered *when* it was not too sensitive, and why it took the Northern Ireland Office over a year to make a decision. One can understand that the needs of 'the media' are pretty low down on the Army's list of priorities, but it is still amazing that those who make these decisions seem to take little account of the wasted time and effort they cause. Researching Northern Ireland had involved numerous visits and a great deal of the TV licence-payer's money to get to the stage where we were ready to film. It must have cost the Ministry of Defence a fair amount as well. The RMP's costs, our transport around the province, and our security were all wasted because it took someone somewhere a full year to decide that Northern Ireland was 'a sensitive matter'.

Apart from our own costs and inconvenience it seemed a shame for the RMP themselves who had wanted us to see some of the specialized work they did there. In many ways, at the time it was their only long-term 'role-in-combat'. Although the Ireland situation was not a real war as such, it did provide the RMP with many similar tasks.

In the event, the series did not need one film entirely dedicated to the province. Now the book provides another opportunity to describe the role of the RMP in Northern Ireland, with, it must be said, an eye on the sensitive nature of the Province and concern for the security of the people who are still working there.

The RMP go out on patrol in support of the RUC. They have been out there doing a policing job and taking the same risks as other British soldiers. They man some border controls and carry out searches of vehicles and their drivers. They become familiar with the 'players' (the IRA) who use the border crossings, and are able to gather a fair amount of low-level intelligence on their comings and goings.

They also play a key role in investigating complaints about the Army. Since there are so many, some have referred to this as a sort of game called 'Army litigation'. The Government

The Queen talking to RMP SSgt Andy Mudd who, aided by a patrolling CP Unit, had saved the life of Sein Fein's Gerry Adams in the early 1980s as a gunman opened fire. Later, in 1989, he lost his leg as the result of an under-vehicle booby trap in Northern Ireland.

has set aside a large amount of money to pay for any injury to a person or his property by the security forces. An element of the population seem to spend a great deal of time making 'complaints' – all of which have to be thoroughly investigated – in the hope of claiming money for an alleged assault or damage of some kind or other. The deadline for a claim is as many as six years after the event.

This means a farmer might claim that an army patrol kicked down his cowshed door five years ago and now he wants to be paid to have it replaced. It may have happened, it may not, but the RMP have to investigate and establish whether it *could* have happened. After extensive checking of records, if it is established that there was a patrol in the vicinity and at the right time then the farmer will be compensated for his loss. However, as one source explained, 'There is no actual proof that the event ever took place. All we are required to do is discover whether it *could* have happened. If it could have happened, there will probably be some kind of payment. It's amazing how often property which people claim has been damaged by the security forces was, let's say, near the end of its useful life anyway.'

One particular claimant was a farmer who had a field of cattle near to a large Army helicopter base. Each time a helicopter took off and flew over the cattle they would run around the field in terror. Since they were beef cattle a lot of running around was having an adverse effect on their weight. Instead of getting fat, they were getting fit. A complaint was made and in the end a fatness/fitness index or table of compensation was devised. At the end of the year, the leaner and fitter the cow, the more money the farmer received to compensate for loss of fat and profit. This must be one of those rare occasions when a conflict brings some benefit for all concerned. The farmer was happy because he got paid for his losses, the Government were happy because they were seen to be taking local grievances seriously and compensating people for the inconvenience caused by the Army – and the cows were happy because they got fit instead of fat. One of those unusual occasions in Ireland when there was nothing to beef about.

Although there has always been a humorous side to the business of 'Army

*Their policing role in
Ireland means that the
RMP are trained to deal
with the dangerous and
unexpected.*

litigation', as with many things there is a darker side as well. Many believe that a large proportion of the claimants are those whose sympathies lie with the IRA. The fact that a fair proportion of the money paid out may go to fund further violence makes the job of trying to establish the validity of claims particularly important. For example, in 1992 the Army paid out a total of £6 million in compensation, and the RMP had to prove that every penny of it was justified.

For the more serious cases of complaint, the RMP are responsible for tracking down and arranging the return of soldiers who have been accused. The average number brought back to face questioning is approximately 3,000 a year. This can mean bringing a soldier back from as far away as the Falklands or even Hong Kong. Since some complaints are up to six years old, the RMP can have considerable difficulty in finding those accused. The RMP spend a great deal of time chasing up last known addresses and working through known relatives.

Not all soldiers want to be found by the Army, especially those who have gone Absent Without Leave or deserted. There are some 5,000 soldiers who are AWOL at any one time. Although a large proportion of these are soldiers who left their units during the Second World War, it still leaves a significant number to work through. Should the RMP's man be one of them the amount of work involved in trying to find him can be considerable. It is thought that the so-called 'diarist' complainants, those who keep a diary of every time they are 'harassed' by the security forces, are well aware of the time and cost involved in returning a large number of soldiers to face complaints, and that this is one of the reasons that the complaints are made.

To help with such a time-consuming task the RMP have developed an extremely efficient information retrieval system which allows them to establish whether soldier A was ever in location B at time C. This information is then used to try and discover whether a complaint is genuine or not.

The RMP also get involved in some of the more unusual cases of adjudication. At one time there was a security system in place at the main entrance to a large military barracks. This system was designed to stop the kind of suicide bomber that caused so much death and destruction in the American embassy in Beruit. The 'lorry stopper' would stop a heavily-laden vehicle piled high with explosives from crashing through the main gate and driving into the heart of the barracks. The main principle of the design was extremely simple. As soon as the guard at the gate thought there was any kind of threat from an approaching vehicle, all he had to do was push a 'crash button'. Upon this command, large concrete bollards would shoot up through the road and disable the lorry or block its path through the gates. Simple, quick and effective. Unfortunately, there were some teething problems.

'We had some technical difficulties which resulted in a few civilian lorries getting written off.' On the occasion the RMP were involved, there had been a lorry delivering a load of wet fish. The bollards were accidentally raised and skewered the lorry. There was a terrible mess – wet fish everywhere and a very cross driver as well. After it had all been sorted out and cleared up, the owner of the lorry put in a claim for £10,000. The RMP decided to investigate.

'One of our top-notch sleuths with a nose for getting to the truth said this claim "smelt a little fishy to him"', so we let him loose on the case.' Their sleuth was indeed correct and after he had established exactly what kind of fish were present in the lorry, the value of the load was reassessed at fifty per cent of the amount claimed. The RMP had saved the Government £5,000 of tax-payers' money and put the owner of the fish back in his plaice!

This was one of those occasions when the 'hearts and minds' policy probably fell on stony ground. This is an 'unofficial' policy explained to us by a senior colonel with considerable experience in the Province. It goes something like this: the Government knows it is getting ripped off with all sorts of bogus claims and that a large proportion of them come from sources likely to support the IRA. Despite this cost, they would rather win the 'hearts and minds' of the average citizen by being seen to bend over backwards to be fair. The logic is that if the Army can be seen to police the situation fairly, then the summary justice meted out by the IRA would compare badly and their support among ordinary men and women would diminish. It is of course impossible to know whether such a policy existed or, if it did, whether it had any effect. What is certain, however, is that without the RMP and their reputation for fairness, any such policy would have been almost impossible to implement.

The RMP have done a great deal of work in the Province and they are respected by both sides for the way they carry out that work. It may well be that if this was one of the ways the Government chose to pursue progress in Northern Ireland and if it did indeed have some effect, then the RMP will have contributed handsomely to the peace that is now being negotiated.

That peace has led to a huge reduction in the corps' most unpleasant task in Northern Ireland – the duties of the coroner's officer. When there have been deaths of Army personnel in bombings, shootings or accidents, it has been the RMP's task to produce a full report of the incident from information given by the pathologist and the scenes-of-crime people. If a body has to be returned to the mainland, the RMP have most of the responsibility for making sure the paperwork is completed correctly and the arrangements are satisfactory.

With its history of violence and danger it is surprising to discover that over 500 retired RMPs choose to stay in the province and buy property there for their retirement. 'It's a wonderful country, the Irish people are great, and the quality of life is brilliant. There's no problem with security, provided you cut your links with the forces when you retire. The IRA go to great lengths to hit "legitimate" targets, so unless you're in and out of GHQ after you retire, you're relatively safe.'

With the reduction of troops in Northern Ireland the need for large numbers of the corps also diminishes. In keeping with their 'first in; last out' tradition it may well be that when the last servicemen leaves the Province he will be a military policeman.

CHAPTER 12

THE FUTURE OF THE RMP

The Provost Marshal (Army) stands at the head of the Royal Military Police. His office is the oldest in the British Army, pre-dating the formation of the military as we know it. Henry Guylford was the first recorded Provost Marshal (PM) in 1511. That says something about the RMP. They are survivors.

The head of the corps, Brig. Iain Cameron, had travelled from his headquarters near Winchester to a small riding stables in Aldershot. He stood in the yard and faced the thirty men and women before him.

'Officers, Troop Sergeant-Major, non-commissioned officers, soldiers of the Royal Military Police Mounted Troop. It is my duty as Provost Martial and Head of Service to officially confirm the disbandment of the Mounted Troop. It will be no consolation to you but I can assure you that everything that could be done was done to preserve the troop and the last working Mounted Unit of the British Army. We failed.'

The troop has a long history with its roots as a fledgling unit going back as far as 1855. Since then it has served in all the British Army's major conflicts. Now it was to be disbanded as part of the 'Front Line First' cost-saving measures introduced by the Government. Someone in Whitehall had to balance his books and so the accountant's pen had scratched off 140 years of history from the payroll.

For the people in the troop it meant something more than an accounting exercise. They were dedicated men and women who lived, ate and slept the troop; for them it was a way of life. Now they sat in the rest room and tried to understand why they had not been spared. One man stared at the floor, 'I've been here eight years now, you couldn't get better job satisfaction for me because it was my hobby as well. I've always loved horses but it's the variety of the thing that I will miss.'

The Army was not just disposing of its mounted policemen it was also disposing of an extremely popular display team. Eight horses combined with as many motorbikes to produce a show which would travel anywhere in the country to perform for the Army or civilians. When they were not employed

The Provost Marshal, Brig. Iain Cameron, with some bad news for the Mounted Troop. The future for the rest of the Redcaps is rosier.

121

in this public relations role they were often asked to bolster security on Army garrisons or add colour and panache to ceremonial events. However, unlike other ceremonial regiments in the Army, the RMP Mounted Troop actually had a full time working function. They patrolled Aldershot Garrisons, policing with a high profile presence.

Wherever there are soldiers, there will be other soldiers to police them, so the future of the Redcaps is inextricably tied up with the future of the British Army. To guess what the Redcaps will look like at the end of the millennium and beyond is the same as asking what on earth is going to happen to the Army. There are one or two pointers.

The highest concentrations of British troops are in Germany and Northern Ireland. But in both theatres two quite cataclysmic events have taken place in recent years that have affected, and will go on affecting, troop levels.

The first was the reunification of Germany in 1990. For forty-five years, West Germany had been the front line against communism. Suddenly there was no enemy. Barracks and airfields were closed or returned to the Germans; troops were disbanded or posted elsewhere. The Army's strength at the time the Berlin Wall came down was 152,800; five years later it is nearer 120,000. This has had an effect on the Redcaps. The police station at Bielefeld is a ghost of what it was, and there is no RMP presence in Celle at all.

The second important development is the ceasefire and 'peace process' in Northern Ireland. This is still at an early stage. At the time of writing we are still barely into the 'talks-about talks' shadow-boxing. Negotiations on the intractable issue of the decommissioning of IRA arms and explosives seem a very long way away. But already the television news has shown pictures of soldiers giving the thumbs-up as they board their RAF flights back to England. Practically all the day-patrolling in Ulster is now carried out by the Royal Ulster Constabulary, and if progress is made on the disarming of the paramilitaries, the trickle of returning soldiers could turn to a flood.

Gazing into the crystal ball, it looks as if the garrison towns of Colchester and Aldershot, and the Army concentrations in Catterick and Salisbury Plain are going to be full of young men, with all the problems that entails for the RMP in the not too distant future.

These two effects of dramatic political change, plus the Chancellor of the Exchequer's need for ever more money, have had the effect of reducing numbers in all three services. Morale is understandably low as each new Government survey – 'Drawdown', 'Options for Change', 'Front line First' – has cut a swathe through the Army, destroying famous regiments, military bands and hallowed traditions in the name of the new gods, Efficiency and Economy. The Redcaps have borne their share with public stoicism and private bitterness.

Attempts have been made by Whitehall to subjugate the Redcaps' identity. In 1992, the Adjutant-General's Corps was formed as an administratively convenient portmanteau for small specialist units like the Royal Army Pay Corps and the Royal Army Education Corps. An attempt was made to subsume the RMP into this amorphous outfit, which partially succeeded. Administratively, the RMP *is* part of the Adjutant-General's Corps (it is easy to rile a Redcap – tell him he is really in the Adjutant-General's Corps) but there was tremendous opposition behind closed doors to a total merging

along the lines of the RAPC and the RAEC, which would have entailed the loss of the cap badge and – perhaps – the red cap itself.

The Redcaps are certainly aware that the enemy is at the gate. An attempt was made in 1994 to move them out of their impressive depot in Chichester to High Wycombe, possibly because Chichester was a valuable piece of real estate. This too was fought off, and with the RMP's computer moving down from London, the depot is safe for two years at least. Looking further afield, outside the UK there are Army units in Antarctica, Ascension Island, Belize, Brunei, Cyprus, the Falkland Islands, Gibraltar, the Gulf and Hong Kong.

In 1997, Hong Kong will be ceded to China. After that date there will be no British troops stationed there, and another glamour posting will have gone. It is anyone's guess what will happen to the other units. But there is a geographical imperative, a centrifugal force that must sooner or later result in the settlement of the Falklands issue, which would then eliminate the need for an Army presence in the staging-post of Ascension Island. Equally, with Britain and Spain members of the European Union, it is hard not to conclude that at some time or another Gibraltar, a relic of Empire, must come to some accommodation with its big neighbour. As for Cyprus, the British forces are tolerated because they are part of the 1960 agreement, and because they are an economic necessity. But nationalist feeling would much rather that the sovereign bases were Cypriot, and it would not take a lot for the pressure to mount as it did in the Philippines, when the Americans were eventually persuaded to vacate their bases at Clark Field and Subic Bay.

Redcaps of the Mounted Troop conceal their feelings, as the full impact of the Provost Marshal's words sink in.

(Above and opposite) The motorbikes and horses of the Mounted Troop display team are applauded enthusiastically at their last police performance.

This dwindling commitment appears to leave little room for a British Army, let alone the RMP. But the hereafter is not totally grim. In the first place the Redcaps have not been culled pro rata. In the latest round of defence cuts, while the Army as a whole suffered a thirty per cent loss, the RMP lost only ten per cent. Secondly, even though the overall trend is for contraction, there are potential growth areas for the Army in general and the RMP in particular.

It is unheard of these days for nation formally and solemnly to declare war on nation. This is the era of the terrorist organization, the nationalist underground, the pressure group with an AK47 up its sleeve. Today an atrocity flashed around the world through satellite on television will bring more publicity to a 'cause' than months and years of patient lobbying in the corridors of the UN. 'Freedom Fighters' with only a scanty knowledge of history need little convincing that 'violence pays'. Close Protection is one of the many roles performed by the RMP. The Redcaps are the bodyguards of military top brass and royalty. There are Redcaps in British embassies throughout the world, where the person of the ambassador and his staff are thought to be under threat. There are Redcaps in the British Embassy in Algiers to protect the ambassador during a very dangerous period of tension between the government of Algeria and Islamic fundamentalists. CP will undoubtedly be a growth area, as the world becomes a nastier and deadlier place.

To the lay observer there is also an unmistakable trend away from national to international solutions to the world's woes, and the world's chief constable is the United Nations, to which Britain has made an unambiguous commitment. British forces are deployed with the UN in Cyprus (UNFICYP), in addition to the already mentioned treaty bases in Kuwait (UNIKOM), and in the former Yugoslavia (UNPROFOR). That these forces may at any time be withdrawn does not alter the fact that a trend has been established.

As long as diplomacy fails, as in Bosnia, there will be pressure to 'bring the boys home', and there are signs that British and French patience is running out. British soldiers, highly trained to engage the enemy, are sitting in tanks and dugouts on twenty-four-hour duty, armed to the teeth, being sniped at, and short of pretty well everything because the roads are closed. Even so, troop contribution to UN forces is cheap. The forces are acquiring practical experience and training in real war or civil war peace-keeping conditions, and at the same time offsetting some of the huge cost of maintaining a standing army. (Estimated defence spending for 1995/6 is £22,130,000,000.) So there is likely to be a continuing, or greater, involvement in UN operations in the years ahead. Apart from anything else, acting in concert with like-minded members will always be more 'politically correct' than unilateral police action.

There is also NATO's Allied Rapid Reaction Corps which is under British leadership. If the order comes to pull out of Bosnia, 40,000 heavily-armed NATO troops from this force would effect an efficient and speedy withdrawal. Alternatively, this NATO army can put up to 100,000 men into the field in any troublespot in the world. The RMP have immense experience in the control of armies on the move, and this expertise would be a godsend in any tactical advance or withdrawal.

There are, then, two forces currently at work that have a bearing on the future of the British Army. The first is the inevitable rundown inherent in the twilight of Empire and the collapse of communism. But counterbalancing this decline is greater involvement in international forces like NATO and the UN, which will ensure a future for a reduced British Army into the twenty-first century. This being so, the red cap is going to be around for many many decades yet.

AGC	Adjutant General Corps
ALS	Army Legal Services
CATPAC	Catering package
CCRIO	Central Criminal Records Information Office
CSM	Company Sergeant Major
DCM	District Court Martial
DIT	Drugs Intelligence Team
FCO	Foreign Commonwealth Office
FUP	Forming Up Point
HIVE	Help Information Volunteer Exchange
HQ	Headquarters
MCTC	Miltitary Corrective Training Centre
MoD	Ministry of Defence
NCO	Non-commissioned Officer
OP	Observation post
PACE	Police and Criminal Evidence Act
Para Provost	Parachute platoon within a provost company
QRH	Queen's Royal Hussars
RMP	Royal Military Police
RSM	Regimental Sergeant Major
RUC	Royal Ulster Constabulary
SAS	Special Air Service
SIB	Special Investigation Branch
Spec Ops	Specialist Operations
SUS	Soldiers under sentence
WO1	Warrant Officer Class 1